PROPHET MUHAMMAD (ﷺ)
As a Planning Expert

Prof Javed Iqbal Saani, PhD

PhD, MBA (MIS), MBA (Finance), BBA

Intellectual Capital Enterprise Limited, London

Copyright © 2017 Prof Javed Iqbal Saani, PhD

All rights reserved.

No reproduction of the book in any form such as electronic, photocopying, scanning, recording or otherwise. It also includes storing for retrieval purposes or transmitting through electronic media i.e., email. Prior written permission of the publisher may require doing any of the above under the relevant act that follows the Copyright, Design, and Patent Act 1988.

Authors and the publisher are not responsible for any damage caused by the application/use of the concepts, techniques, instruction, or actions. The authors and the publisher refuse any implied warranties or related matters.

ISBN 9781974050512

Published by Intellectual Capital Enterprise Limited
ICE Kemp House, 152-160 City Road
London, EC1 V2N
Printed in England

CONTENTS

Dedication	xiii
Acknowledgement	xv
Preface	xvii

1 Introduction   1
- Vision   3
- Mission   4
- Meaning of Planning   5
- Planning the mission   12
- Phase 1: What did he plan?   15
- Premises   17
- The second Phase   19
- Opposition   20
- Planning strategy   22

2 Awareness of Opportunities   25
- Travel to Abyssinia   26
- Islam of Ansaar: The Helpers   28
- The Hijrah   30
- Integration   31
- Truce with Jews   32
- The first armed encounter, the war of Badr   33
- The treaty of Hodabia   35
- The conquer of Makkah   36
- Miscellaneous   37

3 Setting objectives — 41

Objectives of migration to Abyssinia — 46
Treaty of Mina — 47
Objectives of Hijrah — 48
Integration of Migrants and Helpers — 49
Truce with Jews — 50
The first armed encounter, the war of Badr — 51
Objectives of Treaty of Hodabia — 52
Objectives of the conquering of Makkah — 52
Objectives of pre-emptive military and political expeditions — 53
Objectives of correspondence with kings/leaders — 54
Objectives of the journey of Taif — 55

4 Considering planning premises — 57

Travel to Abyssinia — 59
Treaty of Mina — 62
Hijrah expedition — 65
Integration — 67
Treaty with Jews — 70
Treaty of Hodabia — 71
The war of Badr — 73
Makkah under the flag of Islam — 75
Miscellaneous — 76

5 Determining alternatives — 79

Movement to Abyssinia — 79
Journey of Taif — 81
Conquer of Makkah — 82
The prisoners of war of Badr — 83
Battle of Uhad — 85
Banu Nazeer — 86

6 Comparing alternatives courses	*89*
The Hijrah	89
The battle of Uhad	92
Abyssinia	92
Hodabia	93
Integration	95
7 Choosing the most promising one.	*97*
Integration	97
Taif journey	99
The war of Trench	100
Tabuk	101
Hodabia	102
Characteristics of selection	103
8 Formulating the supporting Plans	*105*
9 Quantifying Plans	*115*
10 Implications for Managers	*125*
Planning characteristics	125
Management approach	127
Finance	132
Human resources	134
Bibliography	141
Index	145
About the author	149
Other books by the author (s)	153
Notes	159

Say (to them, O Muhammad): Are those who know equal with those who know not? But only men of understanding will pay heed. [Az-Zumar:9]

Abu'd-Darda' (RA) said, "I heard the Messenger of Allah, may Allah bless him and grant him peace, say,

1. 'Allah will make the path to the Garden easy for anyone who travels a path in search of knowledge.
2. Angels spread their wings for the seeker of knowledge out of pleasure for what he is doing.
3. Everyone in the heavens and everyone in the earth asks forgiveness for a man of knowledge, even the fish in the water.
4. The superiority of the man of knowledge to the man of worship is like the superiority of the moon to all the planets.
5. The men of knowledge are the heirs of the Prophets.
6. The Prophets bequeath neither dinar nor dirham; they bequeath knowledge. Whoever takes it has taken an ample portion.'"

[Abu Dawud and at-Tirmidhi; Riyadh us Salihin, Hadith 1388, p. 211]

Anas (May Allah be pleased with him) reported: The Messenger of Allah (ﷺ) said, "He who goes forth in search of knowledge is considered as struggling in the Cause of Allah until he returns."
[At-Tirmidhi].

Dedication

To my parents who invested heavily for our education and remained engaged in prayers for our success and good being

Acknowledgement

Special gratitude is due to all those who helped me to compile the work. The contribution of my colleague Muhammad Nadeem Khan who was the co-author in one of my previous books for the first exemplar of the present volume is worthwhile.

I am also obliged to my family who spared me to embark on the project. They also provide valuable information which enriched the contents of this effort. May Allah reward them for their contribution? Ameen!

Preface

All prayers to Allah, the exalted, slat wa slam to all the prophets especially upon the last (ﷺ), mercy and blessings upon his noble companions. May Allah (SWT) bestow upon his forgiveness to the entire ummah and ummah of all the prophets (AS). And all those who received the right guidance.

There are numerous dimensions of the life of the prophet (ﷺ) of Islam. And they are emerging with the passage of time and according to the changes that take place in the human requirements. His autobiography coupled with the treasure of hadith and the Quran are the sources of knowledge. The literal work is almost exhausted. However, there is room for analytical work. As a learner of management sciences, I thought some work can be done to gain the pleasure of Allah (SWT). In this connection, I had published an article in 2009 about planning. The Hijrah expedition was the context of analysis.

I thought the work can be extended. Therefore, this project was started. We have applied a model of planning in the previously mentioned article. It seemed appropriate to use the model considering more than one instances. The next question was which instances should be included. I thought those would be appropriate which created distinguished impacts on the mission of the prophet. They were selected which I perceived have influenced the work of dawah because it was the most promising objective of the prophet's (ﷺ) life.

They are: travel to Abyssinia, truce with the Muslims of Madinah, Hijrah, integration of migrants and Helpers, a peace treaty with Jews, the battle of Badr, treaty of Hodabia and the conquer of Makkah. But other instances are also included to expand the scope of input.

The model of planning which is the reference for analysis contains eight dimensions i.e. awareness of opportunities, setting objectives, planning premises, determining alternatives courses, comparing them, choosing the most promising one, making supporting plans and quantify plans.

A chapter is reserved for each of these dimensions where all the instances were related to the dimension of the model. Some other important aspects of the life of the prophet (ﷺ) were also added.

The last chapter deals with the implications which can be extracted from the work. They are arranged in the language of management sciences such as planning characteristics, human resources, finance etc.

It may be worthwhile to say that it is an effort to highlight some aspects of the life of the prophet (ﷺ) about the topic. Keen researchers can expand their understanding to include more dimensions in the analysis. Fundamental purpose is to tell contemporary experts that the concepts of management were grounded in the teachings of Islam that emerged more than fourteen centuries ago. It is believed in the West that the theory of Management emerged with the first treatise that appeared in 1911. We argue that it is not the case it was practiced by our respected prophet(ﷺ) long ago but was not documented. The application of the current model proves that it is true. The prophet (ﷺ) had used the model and did it innovatively. So, he did more than what the model suggests.

I hope the work will be useful for managers and administrators. It may be interesting reading for non-professionals and common readers.

It is an analytical effort; therefore, the emphasis is placed on analysis rather than on the details of the instances. However, necessary details are described to understand the phenomenon.

I pray to Allah, the exalted, to accept the humble effort and make it a source of forgiveness for me and the entire ummah. It may be a source of guidance for readers. Ameen.

Suggestions are welcome so that they may be incorporated in the future editions.

Prof Javed Iqbal Saani, Ph. D

Manchester August 30, 2017

1 Introduction

Going concerns appoint managers to plan organizational matters. The apply well-known approaches for planning either for short-term or long-term. A given authority i.e. board of directors or board of trustees approves their job specification and job descriptions. Managers assume their job according to these factors. Job specification describes the qualification and experience required for a job. The job description describes the details of duties and responsibilities related to the job. We understand that managers duties and responsibilities include planning, organizing, leading, and controlling. The division of duties and responsibilities into these four categories is for the facilitation and understanding of the managerial job.

We are examining a case of managerial activities that prophet (ﷺ) had taken to manage his organization. Allah (SWT) appointed his prophet; He knows the job specifications because He has selected all the prophets (AS). Allah (SWT) has instilled all the requirements or job specifications in the lives of all prophets (AS) and the apostle (AS). Allah (SWT) had taught them "tricks of the trade" as we can see from the life of the prophet (ﷺ). Prophets (AS) used to learn from Allah (SWT) and teach and convey to their nations. Islamic scholars believe that prophets (AS) required two weapons or tools for the job of prophethood: knowledge and strategy. Allah (SWT) bestowed them upon the prophets (AS). Allah (SWT) also described the job descriptions for each of the prophet (AS). He (SWT) trained the prophets (AS) whenever it was necessary. We will discuss them separately in this book; however, this chapter encompasses basics of planning. Plans are linked with and based upon vision and mission of the organisation or its leader. They are discussed before the meaning of planning and associated matters in the following paragraphs.

Vision

The prophet (ﷺ) had an unobstructed vision about his mission. According to the current meaning of the concept, vision is "an aspirational description of what an organization would like to achieve or accomplish in the mid-term or long-term future. It is intended to serve as a clear guide for choosing current and future courses of action." He was appointed to serve the humanity which he visualised and described on many occasions. Once he told to Khabab bin Aret (RA) that be steadfast one-day Allah (SWT) would appoint you the leader of the world. He also predicted the dominance of Islam when Abuzer (RA) took shelter under the umbrella of Islam. He said to go back to your tribe and come back when we would get upper hand. It was the first phase of the Islamic era (the secret period, when dawah was underway in homes and to the near relatives). It came true only after 8 years of the era when the first Islamic state emerged on the globe. And Makkah fell to the hands of Muslims only after 18 years of the period (the first 3 years of the effort).

Mission

Dictionary defines mission as "an organization's core purpose and focus that normally remains unchanged over time ... it serves as filters to separate what is important from what is not, (2) clearly state what will be served and how, and (3) communicate a sense of intended direction to the entire organization." The mission of the prophet (ﷺ) was announced on the first day of open invitation. "O people, I have been sent to warn you about a serious reprimand". He had shown the road map for eternal success. He said, "O people say Allah is one, He is the only deity of worship, and you will be successful." He used both carrot and stick to motivate masses to consider Islam as a way of life. It suggests that his mission was to save mankind through the shield of Islam. History became witnesses that he protected the humanity from eternal disaster. He and his followers earned the respect and dignity in a brief period and became examples for the rest of mankind.

Meaning of Planning

There are some views of experts about the meaning of plan and planning. Let us examine them to gain an understanding of the matter.

Plans are documents that outline how goals are going to be met. They usually include resource allocations, schedules, and other necessary actions to accomplish the goals. As managers plan, they develop both goals and plans.

Planning refers to deciding in advance about the project, product, human resources, and other activities. A manager must address at least five questions about the key areas.

What to do?

When to do?

Where to do?

How to do?

Who will do?

Modern management sciences offer tools, techniques, and strategies to determine each of these effectively and efficiently. These weapons were not developed at the time of the prophet (ﷺ) but he and his team have applied them. For instance, Iqbal and Ahmad (2009) have examined a planning strategy with respect to Hijrah expedition. They have applied a well-known strategy or planning model suggested by modern experts. Surprisingly, the prophet (ﷺ) had utilized all the steps involved in his Hijrah from Makkah to Madinah. It suggests that the same model can be applied to another example we are going to put forward here. For example, one of the current experts defines planning as it "is a complex form of symbolic action that consists of consciously preconceiving a sequence of actions that will be sufficient for achieving a goal. It is set apart from un-deliberated action, which is not preconceived." (Pea, 2015) And the other simplifies it as "Planning is preparing a sequence of action steps to achieve some specific goal" (Time Management Guide, 2015). The goal of the noble team was to reach Madinah for which they had undergone a series of steps. The steps were so accurate and effective that they had achieved their goals without interruption.

The prophet (ﷺ) has managed a range of endeavours: business, management of migration, management of wars, and management of treaties. He has managed his business prior to the announcement of his prophethood. His foreign business trips were successful and generated a handsome profit for the parties concerned. The business partnership converted onto a life partnership with the business colleague. Here we can assume that he has done something special which produced extraordinary results. Thus, he was a successful business manager even if he had applied only privileged business techniques. It is because the outcome determines the success of any strategy; if it is known but not being applied than the experts suggest that it should be applied. For instance, the prophet's (ﷺ) honesty was famous; it might be one of the causes of success, but everyone was not applying it.

Since the migration from Makkah to Madinah was the most illustrious incident in the history of Islam and in fact in the history of the world because the incident transformed the fate of people for ever, therefore, it seems appropriate to describe it in planning perspective.

The planning for it was started when the prophet (ﷺ) invited the delegates of Madinah towards Islam during the Hajj. Fortunately, some of them embraced his message. A larger group took shelter under the shade of Islam later. When they came to know that Muslims were in hardship in Makkah, they invited them to Madinah to avoid the difficulties they were facing. Muslims started to leave Makkah individually or in small groups to avoid an open battle with the infidels. The prophet (ﷺ) left when most of the companions reached Madinah.

The journey itself was an example of a well-planned venture. Abu Bakker prepared two she camels for the journey; they travelled in a team which was formed prior to departure. The guide was hired, and the new path was adopted. The team stayed in the cave Saur for three days to divert the attention of the enemy who was searching for them actively. The expedition seemed a well-planned endeavour which was successful.

In addition, the prophet (ﷺ) has led 27 battles where he participated himself. All were won. Three factors were required for a war: Human resources, weapons and working capital i.e. day to day necessities. In addition, a strategy was also required to utilize these resources. As an example, on Badr, he has appointed a sahabi to look after the affairs of Madinah and took everyone else with him. When Tabuk was to be conducted announcement was made for the preparation and donation were collected. The preparation was to be made by those who supposed to participate in terms of the weapons and necessary provision. There was no collective programme of training at that time. It was the part of a child grooming that he learns how to use sword, arrow, and other prevalent armours. In this way, every soldier was 'home trained'. However, the prophet (ﷺ) used to keep extra weapons. It is reported that 12 swards were in his possessions at the time of his eternal departure.

The third type of projects the prophet (ﷺ) dealt with was the political negotiation and arriving at appropriate treaties. Planning was made when it was thought as an individual or in the team i.e.

called shurah about the issue. It is followed by the formal communication with the tribe concerned. So, a conversation was to start to decide the terms and conditions of the proposed pact.

There would be internal meetings of the shurah or sub committees who used to write terms of reference and to propose the team members who would negotiate and write dawn the agreement. It suggests that there was a system to do all these activities and to manage them.

Robins and Coulter (2011) split the planning into three parts: decision making, planning, and strategic management. They believe planning means "defining the organization's goals, establishing strategies for achieving those goals, and developing plans to integrate and coordinate work activities. It is concerned with both ends (what) and means (how). According to DeCenzo & Robbins (2010) planning consists of two elements: goals and plan. For him "Goals (objectives) are desired outcomes or targets." He says, "They guide management decisions and form the criterion against which work results are measured. That is why they are often described as the essential elements of planning. Managers must know the desired target or outcome before you can establish plans for reaching it." The goal (objective) of the prophet (ﷺ) are discussed in chapter 4.

Planning the mission

We can divide planning endeavours into two phases: the Makken phase and the Madinah phase. An alternative division is possible i.e. short-term and long-term. It may be contrary to the current meaning of the planning phases which include short-term as any planning up to one year and long term beyond it. Some use medium term-planning that covers more than one year but less than three years. Anyway, whatever period one uses for planning or understanding it, it is relating to the achievement of the objective.

We have used Makken and Madinah period because the range of objectives varied during these periods. The prophet (ﷺ) had expanded the message of Allah at the individual level. For example, he invited people towards Allah individually in Makkah while he invited the rulers of other countries as a head of the state in Madinah. He fought wars with opponents as a collective group while in Makkah he and his followers were persecuted individually. The opponents made many efforts to eliminate the entire Muslim community in Makkah but one by one not at once as they had done in the formal wars later. Their purpose was to harm the prophet (ﷺ) so that when he would not be there than his followers would disappear or leave the new religion. Nevertheless, every Muslim when entered in the fold of Islam became determined to die as Muslim irrespective of when.

There was another example of such feelings. When Bilal (RA) received persecution from disbelievers, there were no collective efforts on the part of the Muslim community to rescue him. Abu Bakar (RA) bought his freedom. However, it was possible that he would have done it from the instruction of the prophet (ﷺ). Similarly, Yasir (RA) and his family received great loss from the infidels, but no one took collective action against them. This was the Will of Allah (SWT); He has not instructed them to take revenge. However, collectively was there. Muslims made two migrations to Abyssinia in groups and the prophet (ﷺ) made Hijrah with Abu Bakker (RA).

The strategy of dawah was individual, the prophet (ﷺ) used to invite people on a one-o-one basis. The programme consisted of four phases:

1. From the beginning to the third year of year of the prophet (YP)

2. From the third year to fifth YP

3. From year 5 to year 10 YP

4. From year 10-13 YP

We examine them in turn.

Secret promotion of his idea (secret plan)

From a managerial perspective, a product includes physical artefacts, services, and ideas. The prophet (ﷺ) was promoting a new idea (It was new for the sake of argument, however, as the Qura'n says to the nearest effect, Islam was the original name of the heavenly religion, but people change its name according to their own will i.e. Christianity etc.), Islam.

Phase 1: What did he plan?
The prophet (ﷺ) put forward the new idea to his household, his loyal wife in the first instance. It was like test marketing. He proceeded to the close friend and a respectful personality of the city and Quraysh, Abu Bakker. In the second phase, the prophet (ﷺ) gathered Quraysh and presented the idea to them. He announced that

Allah (SWT) had appointed him as a prophet (ﷺ); I testify that Allah (SWT) is one, there is no deity of worship except him. I invite you to accept it as I believe it. You would be successful in this world and will be honoured in the Hereafter. His argument was to ask people to embrace his as a prophet (ﷺ) and accept the supremacy of Allah (SWT) as the only to whom one should worship. He invited towards one Allah because most of the people were worshipping multi gods, they were a polytheist.

There were a couple of things to do to introduce the new idea gradually.

1. First was to sell the new idea (product) to people (in business language to the new customers).

2. Second to educate them.

3. Third to keep them motivated to continue to own the new product.

4. Fourth to ask them to sell the idea to others.

5. People of the surrounding areas would listen about the new idea; they would come to embrace the idea. How to deal with them?

Premises

He started 'work from home' but it was not sufficient to educate existing and newcomers and hold meetings to promote the product. Education was necessary to explain the way the new idea is to use /practice. Similarly, new revelations were comping from Allah (SWT); they were supposed to convey to those who had adopted the product. It was a source of motivation for everyone, it was also authenticating the prophethood of the presenter. Some of them were descending according to the circumstances that emerged with the passage of time. For instance, surah Lahab was revealed as an answer to the actions of Abu Lahab and his wife.

Therefore, a separate place was chosen to work as an office. It was near the Holy Masjid, inside the neighbourhood. People used to enter the street and could enter the home secretly. It was known as 'Home of Arqum (RA)'. The place was also appropriate for those who were travelling from nearby areas in search of the new religion (product). When a new product is introduced, people want to know it. So, it was the demand of the time to sell them the product and educate them or train them how to use it.

The prophet (ﷺ) and his companions used this academy as a centre for learning. Salat was introduced during this period. Existing and newcomers learned it here. Since it was the meeting place, therefore, the new revelation was also announced in the home. The work of invitation towards the new religion was, however, secret. The prophet (ﷺ) and companions used to visit prospective people in their homes, or they were brought to the academy where the prophet (ﷺ) was explaining them, Islam. Hazrat Umer

(RA) became Muslim in the home of Arqum (RA). Abuzer Ghaffari became Muslim here, for instance.

The second Phase

Allah (SWT) ordered to start the work of dawah openly now. It was logical to keep the message secret for a while so that some dignitaries should accept it. The part of the plan was to inject the idea slowly. When it would be presented openly, some supporters should be there who can help, if necessary. Once people were making a quarrel with the prophet and Abu Bakker (RA) helped him to get rid of infidels. The existence of other Muslims was also a motivational technique for the newcomers. They were referred to that your kin men and women already embraced it. When Umer was heading to harm the prophet (ﷺ), he was referred to the Islam of his sister. It meant that it was a practical idea, not an abstract philosophy. In business strategy, new products especially medicines are tested on a limited scale in a controlled manner prior to commercialization. Islam was in the process of "commercialisation", so open "sales" of the product was preceded with a secret introduction.

Opposition

In the management world or business world, stronger or established companies compete with the emerging organisation. They increase promotional budget, change characteristics of their products to match the competing ones. Sometimes it does not work; they start price war i.e. reducing the prices of their products to attract customers. The new comer or niche marketers have to react to maintain the customer base. Many big companies eliminate competition through acquisition. They buy a new product with its owners. Similar was the situation in Makkah.

The disbelievers also started a cold war against the new religion. They wanted to isolate the prophet (ﷺ) from his clan so that they can fulfil their mal intentions. In the first instance, they tried to bargain, give, and take. Although the prophet (ﷺ) always like it and adopted the soft side of a solution. He did it at the occasion of prisoners of war, Badr. He liked the soft suggestions of Abu Bakker (RA) against the hard arguments of Umer (RA). He embraced all the unfavourable conditions of Quraysh for the treaty of Hodabia. However, there was always a borderline. When Quraysh offered material benefits in lieu of relinquishing his mission. He decisively announced, "if they put the sun in my one hand and the moon in the other hand, I would not forsake my job because I have been appointed for it." The Divine answer also descended to him.[1] It strongly rejected any chance of a bargain. The opponents were plainly

---

[1] Say: O disbelievers! I worship neither that which you worship; nor worship you that which I worship. And I shall not worship that which you worship. Nor will you worship that which I worship. To you your religion, and to me my religion. [Kafirun: 1-6]

informed, you do whatever you can do but I shall continue my job as usual.

Planning strategy

There were a lot of occasions when Muslims had to defend themselves. We examine here some of them to identify the planning strategy of the prophet (ﷺ). We will investigate the war of Badr, Uhad, Khanduq, Fatah Makkah, and Tabuk. We have included them because they are important for their impact on the life of Muslims and competing parties. For instance, the first one decided the fate of Quraysh. But we need to identify its features related to planning. They are.

1 It was a defensive plan which was made as a contingency way of action. The Islamic troops were not meant to fight. They were forced to do so.

Since the venue of action was an away match, therefore, the choice was limited in terms of resources and venue.

3- Allah, the exalted decided the outcome, the prophet (ﷺ) resort to Him. The Divine help produced the result. We believe that He makes all decisions with resources or without them. His plan was to succeed, no one could change it.

4- The opponents were proud of their number and equipment. It implies investing more resources is not the guarantee for success. A better strategy can beat it. And it happened.

5- It was the first experience of the prophet (ﷺ) as a military leader. He did not attend any cadet college but demonstrated the qualities of an expert. It was evidence of his prophethood.

2 Awareness of Opportunities

Let us look at the event from a planner's perspective. Iqbal and Ahmad (2009) applied a planning model on the Hijrah expedition. It seems appropriate to evaluate this plan as well on the bases of similar premises.

As a planning expert, one needs to identify the reasons for planning. He identifies the opportunities for which plan can be made. Let us investigate the life of the prophet (ﷺ) and the opportunities he had identified. Although all events and expeditions were important, we have included eight of them which had created an especially significant role in the spread of His message. They are:

1. Travel to Abyssinia
2. Pact with people of Madinah

3. Migration to Madinah
4. Integration of Migrants and Helpers
5. Truce with Jews
6. The first armed encounter, the war of Badr
7. Treaty of Hodabia
8. Conquer of Makkah

The analysis is based on these events but sometimes the author cannot find a particular reference in any of these so other instances is included. Sometimes, relevant material was not available out of these instances even, so the only available part is applied.

Travel to Abyssinia

The plan starts with awareness of opportunity because of the environmental scan. Since we are examining a case which already had occurred, therefore, we need to identify the issues which lead to the decision. If we look at the situation, we can say that there were three issues on the table:

1 How to protect existing companions?

2   How to practice Islam independently?
3   How to expand the idea?

Koontz and his colleague (2006) believe that a planner needs to dig out the opportunities. For instance, expansion of operations in the existing or new markets. As far as the phenomenon was concerned the existing market exhausted and the development was terribly slow. However, expansion in other markets or more specifically in other geographical areas was possible. The environmental scan showed that there are four geographical areas: Abyssinia, Taif, Madinah, and rest of Arab lands.

The prophet (ﷺ) *considered* Abyssinia because the king was a just ruler and he was practicing his religion religiously. The country was away from Makkah so there was a minimum chance of any interference from Quraysh. Under the protection of the proposed country, Muslims could practice their faith openly and freely. When Muslims arrived in the country, they had demonstrated Islam practically and verbally. We understand that a delegation of Quraysh followed them and complained to the king of Abyssinia. Muslims were summoned to the royal court, and they presented Islam effectively. It created impacts on the king who became Muslim later. It suggests that the right opportunity was identified.

Islam of Ansaar: The Helpers

The next opportunity he had identified become the most promising for him and his message. That was the people of Madinah. Albeit he could visit their area, but it was far from Makkah, his area of current activity. He thought they could be approached at the time of hajj. It was year 5 Nabvi when six persons accepted his invitation. It preceded one of the major events of the century i.e. the formal truce between the prophet (ﷺ) and the new Muslim community of Yasrib. It laid down the foundation for the treaty of bait-e-uqba --saniya (the second treaty of Mina). Muslims of Madinah formally invited the prophet (ﷺ) to shift his activities to their home land. It took him about three months to implement the truce.

Madinah was the home of Jews who were the holder of the book and shared the oneness of Allah, the exalted with Muslims. The tribe of Khizraj and Aows were also important because they were significant in number, they knew the divine books and the reality of prophethood due to social relations with Jews. Jews were waiting for a prophet (ﷺ) to come so these tribes as well. Sowaid bin Samat was a poet and an influential person amongst them once he travelled for hajj and met the prophet (ﷺ). Exchanged words with him and received the positive impact of Islam and the prophet (ﷺ). A delegation of the leaders of Aows approached the Quraysh for a possible military alliance after the war of Baath where the tribe received a crushing defeat of arch rival Khizraj. Quraysh refused to go ahead but the prophet (ﷺ) talked to them and invited them to take refuge under the tent of Islam. The leader of the delegation did not agree but other members got effected. Madinah was attractive because its people were visiting Makkah for hajj so it was easy for the prophet (ﷺ) to develop relations with them. The sixth sense of the prophet (ﷺ) also indicated him to consider them. It suggests that there were opportunities in Madinah for expansion of the 'market' to introduce the new product.

The Hijrah

Another illustrious land mark of his management skills was planning and implementation of hijra expedition. As for as identification of the opportunities was concerned it was the "game change" discovery of opportunities. However, it resulted as an outcome of the treaty with the people of Madinah. He was in search of a place where the base camp of the whole activity may be shifted but any appropriate venue was not found yet. He travelled to Taif for this purpose and sent two delegations to Abyssinia to find out such a place. Nevertheless, it was destined for the people for Madinah. They deserved it. The hospitality they have shown to the prophet (ﷺ) and his companion of Makkah was nothing less than unprecedent peace of sacrifice. With the Divine guidance, he travelled the journey to reach the perfect place which served his headquarters for the rest of his life and beyond.

Integration

When he stepped in the new land, many his colleagues already arrived there from Makkah. They left their homes for the pleasure of Allah, the exalted. They needed shelter, food, and work to survive in the new land. The prophet (ﷺ) identified another opportunity to integrate them with the local community. He has established it through a remarkable action commonly known as the establishment of "brotherhood". It was done on one-to-one basis. His far-reaching thinking capability dug out the opportunity to induct the new comers with existing "employees". The Helpers or ansaar honoured it generously but the migrants were also the sons of elites. They accepted it as a last resort. Most of them were traders so they took the way of markets and started to stand on their feet soon. The Helpers offered them their homes and gardens. Soon after the migration, both groups integrated into a single nation, the Muslims. Not only that after eight years the Makkans were over overcome but there was no single instance that the migrants went back to Makkah. The left it for the pleasure of Allah (SWT) and his prophet (ﷺ) so they stuck with it. At the time of Badr, they have already demonstrated that there were no blood relations, there was no geographical affiliation and what was there, the relation of Islam.

Truce with Jews

Having been established the internal security and cooperation, the prophet (ﷺ) had found out the possibility of an external threat. It could emerge from the neighbours who did not solicit the protection of the new religion. It was possible through a political initiative. He took the first step and proposed them (the Jewish community) for the cooperation. At last, a formal agreement was signed for the establishment of the collaboration. It was a social binding and a military alliance. Although Jewish did not honour it for a long time from the Muslims perspective it was victory without war.

The first armed encounter, the war of Badr

The prophet (ﷺ) adopted a strategy to engage Quraysh in small episodes to gain control over their trade route because Quraysh had expelled them form their homeland, captured their properties and were making conspiracy to eliminate them. They travelled towards Madinah to show their intent. The prophet (ﷺ) came to know about a big caravan which was in control of Abu Sufyan. Since it was carrying goods which needed many personnel, therefore, the prophet (ﷺ) took a large group with him for the campaign. The first purpose was to capture it which might be done with a small armed encounter and to collect and bring merchandise etc. Therefore, the prophet (ﷺ) had selected an enormous number of people with him. Since it was with the permission of Allah, the exalted, thus He knew what would happen. He promised success to Muslims either capture of the caravan or a victory in the encounter. The prophet (ﷺ) had found it an opportunity to enjoy His bounty.

As for as its impacts were concerned, it was a game change episode. The history witnessed the importance of it; it changed the fate of the world not to speak the life of Muslims. Quraysh found it a crushing defeat and an unexpected event. Look at this piece of history. After the defeat, the Quraysh sent an informer to disseminate the shocking news for their doom. One of the sons of a chieftain of Quraysh was sitting in Hateem (an external part of the holy mosque) the informer told people about the murder of his father and a brother. He said to people about the informer, he seems to me a mad person. Ask him about me whether I had been killed. The informer replied he was sitting there.

The treaty of Hodabia

The prophet (ﷺ) had identified another opportunity which created an impression on the human kind. Muslims delayed accelerating the efforts of the prosperity of Islam. It caused to recognise the political power of Islam. Quraysh was pushed in the closed street. Open mixing with Muslims enables them to know the character of Islam. All that was achieved through the treaty of Hodabia. Allah (SWT) made the real plans and ordered his prophet (ﷺ) to go for Umrah. The prophet (ﷺ) got prepared with 1400 companions to travel to the holy land, but infidels stopped them. The prophet's (ﷺ) far reaching strategy worked and the journey ended at Hodabia rather than in Makkah with a political truce. Muslims had to return but Allah, the exalted, called it a success. Muslims retreated upon the promise of Allah (SWT), but they gained a lot. The prophet (ﷺ) turned a threat (a war for which his companions were also ready) into an opportunity. He gained it with peaceful means.

The conquer of Makkah

The prophet (ﷺ) had generated another fantastic opportunity out of a mistake of his opponents. A prudent planning expert always keeps a keen eye on the activities of his competition. Whenever it is viable, he takes advantage of it. A confederate clan of Quraysh killed many men of a Muslims' confederate clan called Khaza. They approached the prophet (ﷺ) and ask for help. The prophet (ﷺ) sent an envoy to Quraysh and asked them to pay the blood money or separate themselves from the guilty clan or Muslims would consider the treaty of Hodabia cancelled. Quraysh accepted the last provision in the first instance but when thought seriously, tried to renew the treaty but the "will of god was done". Muslims rejected to restore the treaty. The prophet (ﷺ) had started preparations for the final and decisive episode. After about eight years of his expulsion from the city, Allah, the exalted has returned him victorious. While he was entering in Makkah, he was saying Allah (SWT) has done it alone. He has helped his slave. The right has come and the wrong has gone, surly the wrong to go.

Miscellaneous

The prophet (ﷺ) has also visualised the targets after gaining stability. The Kings and tribal leaders had an influence on their subjects. The prophet (ﷺ) had tried in Taif and other places. They were the opinion leaders; their acceptance could motivate their subjects to follow them. Tofail Dhosi and others had already made an impact upon their people.

Since they were large in number, so it was not practical to approach them individually. Many ambassadors were deputed. The prophet (ﷺ) communicated through written means. Many responded positively. Some showed hostility. From a planning perspective, it was an extraordinary step to deliver what was expected. It also strengthened his vision to reach everyone to convey/introduce his idea. It is worthwhile to mention that all these were peaceful measures. Islam believes in peace and always wanted to make efforts for it. The prophet (ﷺ) picked the sward as the last resort. One non-Muslim author said Islam, has humanized the war. It was true from the life of the prophet (ﷺ) who brought a revolution with the sacrifice of only 900 lives.

The prophet has identified many opportunities for propagating his idea. Allah, the exalted, was guiding him. As a human being, he wanted to start with his family members who needed it urgently because they were on the wrong path. Allah, the exalted, ordained him, warn those people whose forefathers were not warned.[2] They were warned in two phases: started work secretly and then after about three years, openly. It was a wonderful opportunity; the prophet (ﷺ) spent a lion share of his efforts upon his family.

<u>Taif</u> was the home of a tribe of large in number. The number was an important parameter of

---

[2] That you may warn a folk whose fathers were not warned, so they are heedless. [Yaseen: 6]

success at the time. Two heads were better than one. The city was near Makkah; prophet (ﷺ) could reach conveniently. He wanted to extend his scope of authority to <u>Taif</u> because he believed there was a large tribe; it was strong in military terms and thus, had influence in the area. For him, it was so important that he decided to visit himself. His visit did not produce an immediate outcome but later, the people of the city took shelter under the umbrella of Islam.

After the *war of Trench*, the prophet (ﷺ) has articulated an offensive plan. He found out another opportunity to strengthen his mission. This time he intended to perform Umrah. It was a religious activity apparently but there were other objectives to achieve. He had to demonstrate his might because the war of Trench was a technical victory. The united army could not crush Muslims to death. They were restricted to launch an all-out offensive due to the Trench. And there was a meagre chance of victory; if one analyses from the point of the number of personnel involved in the combat, the ratio was like that of Badr where they were beaten.

3 Setting objectives

We are discussing the life of the prophet (☫) in managerial perspective in the contemporary environment, hence, we need to understand the phenomenon in current circumstances. I mean the primary target of the book is a manager who understands the managerial language. Therefore, we arrange the material accordingly. And we will solicit the help of contemporary experts of the field to do so. For instance, according to Decenzo (2011) planning consists of two elements: goals and plan. For him "Goals (objectives) are desired outcomes or targets." He says, "They guide management decisions and form the criterion against which work results are measured. That is why they are often described as the essential elements of planning. Managers must know the desired target or outcome before you can establish plans for reaching it."

So, let us see what the goals of the prophet (ﷺ) were (remember that Allah (SWT) has defined the goals). The first goal was to learn or learn how to read. Allah (SWT) has described goals for the prophet (ﷺ).

1- "Read: In the name of your Lord Who creates, creates man from a clot." [Al-`Alaq: 1-2].

2- O thou wrapped up in thy raiment! Keep vigil the night long, save a little [Al-Muzammil: 1-2]

3- So, remember the name of thy Lord and devote thyself with a complete devotion [Al-Muzammil: 8]

4- And bear with patience what they utter, and part from them with a fair leave - taking. [Al-Muzammil: 10]

5- And seek forgiveness of Allah. [Al-Muzammil: 20]

However, the most important responsibility/objective was:

O you enveloped in your cloak, arise, and warn! Your Lord magnifies, your raiment purifies, pollution shuns! [Al-Muddaththir:1]

Allah (SWT) defined personal objectives in the first instance 1-5 above (Nevertheless, it is not an exhaustive list). And then He assigned a grand objective. Personal objectives which turn into qualities and functioned as weapons/tools to achieve the grand objective. The prophet (ﷺ) was determined to achieve the objective. When Abuzer (RA) embraced Islam, the prophet (ﷺ) advised him to keep your Islam secret and announce it when we would get upper hand. Once his daughter was worried about him, the prophet (ﷺ) condoled her and said, "do not worry, your father's religion would enter every home one day" On another occasion the disbeliever who perceived that the prophet (ﷺ) was offering a new religion to gain some worldly objectives. So, they offered wealth, leadership and women in lieu of stopping the job of dawah (Even many people believe the same today regarding the people who do some work of dawah). The prophet (ﷺ) rejected their offer and said if they put the sun on my one hand and the moon, on the other hand, I would not stop this work.

Allah (SWT) had also assigned an associated objective:

And give glad tidings (O Muhammad) to those who believe and do good works; that theirs are Gardens underneath which rivers flow; as often as they are regaled, with food of the fruit thereof, they say: This is what was given us a foretime; and it is given to them in resemblance. There for them are pure companions; there forever they abide. [Al-Baqarah:25]

Some of the glad tidings include:

- Accept Islam you would get success in this world and in the Hereafter.

- Pray salat (Namaz) and receive forgiveness

- Pay zakat and purify your money

- Fast in Ramadan and get taqwa i.e. Nearness to Allah (SWT)

- Do hajj and be rich (Ghani)

- Forgive others and get honoured

It suggests the key objective was to invite people towards Islam e.g.

Say: This is my way: I call on God with sure knowledge, I and whoever follows me – Glory be to God! And I am not of the polytheists. [Yusuf: 108]

Allah (SWT) assigned the same mission/objective to all prophets (AS). Allah planned the way to achieve it and the prophet (ﷺ) implemented it. Given the above objectives let us look at some of the objectives he had articulated for his major projects.

His grand objective was to spread Islam in four corners of the world. Allah, the exalted had assigned it to him. The purpose was to save humanity from eternal disaster and show them the path of success in this world and in the Hereafter.

Objectives of migration to Abyssinia

In response to the persecution of Quraysh, the prophet (ﷺ) had decided to send some of his companions to Abyssinia. The purpose was to seek a safe place for them where they could practice Islam freely and propagate it. They could stay there until a way out might be found. Therefore, these migrants joined Muslims in

Madinah when the prophet (ﷺ) himself migrated to the city.

Treaty of Mina

Since the prophet (ﷺ) was in search of a place where the headquarter may be shifted yet could not find until the people of Madinah started to embrace Islam. As we know the first group of many people secretly took the oath of obedience in the year 10 Nabvi; the second group followed them. They also made a covenant to work for Islam on the way back to their home town. The prophet (ﷺ) sent a delegate to promote the religion and teach to those who accept the message. The effects were useful and chieftain level people came under the umbrella of Islam. It made it possible for the Muslims of Madinah to travel for hajj in substantial number.

The first objective was the spread of Islam; it was the primary objective of the prophet (ﷺ). He wanted to save everyone from the fire of Hell. Remember when he first time invited Quraysh towards Islam, he said to accept my message you would get success. The letter he wrote to the king of Persia says, it is my responsibility as a prophet (ﷺ) of Allah (SWT) to warn people about the bad end.

The second purpose was to find out a new place where he could transfer his base camp. The treaty of Mina paved the way for it. It became the predecessor for Hijrah which achieved the objective. The people of Madinah took the prophet (ﷺ) for good.

Objectives of Hijrah

Hajrah was one of the major moments in the life of the prophet (ﷺ). The objective of the Hijrah was to spread Islam freely in the new land. Makkans were unable to stop him or his companions to do so. Muslims were also safe of their hostility. The prophet (ﷺ) established the first Islamic state in Madinah which was the ultimate objective of his life so that organised efforts should be made for the success of his mission. He established Islam as a way of life. A structured system was developed to manage the affairs of the state. (IIPH, 1999).

Integration of Migrants and Helpers

Safe arrival in Madinah necessitated ensuring peace and security in the city and the surrounding areas. The first step was to integrate the two communities, Mohajreen and Ansaar. The purpose was to break the tribal system and replace it with the Islamic values. Islam brought leaders and common people to together. They were standing in slat in the single row; they needed to integrate into a single family. The purpose was to create a new culture where people were recognised through "fear of Allah and nearness to Him" rather than tribal affiliation. Thus, the tribal relationship must be replaced with the religious relationship. The objective was to create a social community that extends its scope to economic activity and beyond. The migrants had left everything behind, but they did not want to live as dependents. They, however, required temporary support to stand on their feet. They harvested it through the creation of brotherhood. The prophet (ﷺ) has achieved the objective, and it was a great achievement, the example of which the known history cannot present.

Truce with Jews

Jews of Madinah were strong and influential, especially when comparing with the Helpers. They were less in number and were not United. So weak and dispersed. The migrants were rare. It was the demand of the time to take a bold political step. The prophet (ﷺ) did it. He invited Jews and Helpers and commenced dialogue for a peace treaty. The prophet (ﷺ) did it on equal footing especially Jews were bound not to make an alliance with Quraysh. Both parties shall stand together in case of any external aggregation. They shall join any future treaty together. It shows that the terms of the treaty were in favour of Muslims. The objective was to gain political stability and a military confederation for a strong defence. Also, to demonstrate the existence of a new power in Madinah.

The first armed encounter, the war of Badr

The prophet (ﷺ) wanted to get engaged with surrounding tribes especially with Quraysh. He wanted to implement his vision i.e. spreading of Islam in four corners of the world. However, Quraysh was one of the major impediments for achieving it. Allah, the exalted, indicated success soon. In pursuance of the bounty the prophet (ﷺ) tried to block the trade rout of Quraysh. Small expeditions were sent to warn Quraysh in a row. However, a bigger and decisive initiative was absent. The purpose was to be to send a strong message to the opponents about the existence of a new power in the North. Although the war was not an objective at the time of the encounter Quraysh travelled about 300 km to crush Muslims. Muslims had to defend themselves despite they were not well armed, and their intention was not to fight a war when they left Madinah. Nevertheless, the "they will be god was done". Allah (SWT) wanted to give a victory to his obedient servants and teach a lesson to the chronic dis-believers.

Objectives of Treaty of Hodabia

As we know the importance of the treaty of Hodabia; its objectives were significant in the journey of success. The first one was to fulfil the command of Allah, the exalted which was conveyed through a dream. The second objective was to prevent the "Quraysh-Khyber" alliance according to As-Sallaabee (2006) was about to happen. In addition, according to Arab tradition, Makkah was a free city; no one has the right to prevent any one to perform Umrah, but Quraysh acted against it which created moral support for Muslims, and unexpected gain.

Objectives of the conquering of Makkah

"It is the day of Kabah", the prophet (ﷺ) proclaimed while entering in Makkah in 8 A.H. as a victorious general. Muslims achieved several objectives. Overcome the chronic resistance, demonstrated that the rule of Islam would prevail now. Guilty was forgiven, the hearts of Makkans were won and they were gifted generously. Their lands and belongings were kept with them. No women were made a slave and so on. The flag of Islam was installed on the top of Kabah for ever. It was the predecessor of Muslim dominance in the centuries to come. All of that was the example of ambitious objectives. And they sustained it.

Objectives of pre-emptive military and political expeditions

Molana Nadvi (2005) writes about the pre-emptive military and political expeditions of the prophet (ﷺ) in year 1 and 2 AH. The purpose was to develop political relations with surrounding tribes to prevent Makkans to make an alliance with these people which could be a danger for the Muslims. It also included challenging the military power of Quraysh, made their trade routes vulnerable, restricting their movements and to increase the influence of the new power. Another objective was to get prepared for a formal and bigger encounter. They were the prototype of the actual product. The prophet (ﷺ) had defined and implemented these small episodes where internal and external management of resources, intelligence management, consistency and frequency of events were some of the objectives achieved. The prophet (ﷺ) did not want war at this occasion, but he intended to improve economic blockade and to enhance military and political influence on the neighbouring tribes.

Objectives of correspondence with kings/leaders

As we have mentioned in the awareness of opportunities in the previous chapter; when Islam started to flourish in and around Madinah, the prophet (ﷺ) planned to reach Kings and leaders of neighbouring Arabs. The objective was to take the first step towards expansion through peaceful measures. Kings and tribal leaders were invited to embrace Islam. Explicitly it was a soft message to the recipients to take refuge under the umbrella of Islam.

Alternatively, other means would be applied to reach them. It was also an announcement that a new political and military power has emerged in Madinah. The response was mixed; some respected and others did not pay heed. Some took shelter under the flag of Islam, and some appreciated. As-Sallaabee (2006) believes the purpose was to know their response to develop the political and military strategy to deal with them. [3]

Objectives of the journey of Taif

The prophet (ﷺ) was in search of a place where the headquarter may be shifted since year 5 of Nabvi. Nevertheless, the appropriate place was not found. Five years later the prophet (ﷺ) planned to visit Taif, a neighbouring town of Sakeef. Its purpose was to identify an alternative destination. Also, to invite the people of the city towards Islam. It was a journey of deferred success i.e. which was not immediate.

---

[3] As-Sallaabee, Ali Muhammad (2006) The Noble Life of the Prophet, peace be upon him.

It was like the treaty of Hodabia which was called "an implied success". According to Molana Nadvi (2005),[4] the prophet (ﷺ) entered Makkah with the protection of a clan called Khaza which was opposing Quraysh regarding the prophet (ﷺ) and was supporting Muslims since the inception of Islam. Matum bin Addi was the head of the clan, he asked his troops to get armed and announce in the holy mosque about the protection. Thus, the Quraysh were divided into two groups. It was a strategic move and the achievement of a long-term objective. It is the same clan whose members were killed which caused the end of the Hodabia treaty. And Muslim advance towards Makkah in year 8 AH.

---

[4] Nadvi (2005)

4 Considering planning premises

It is the assumptions about the environment according to Koontz and Heinrich (2006) about a range of parameters including social and political conditions that prevailed in the society. They varied at various times. Let us look at some of them.

When the prophet (ﷺ) launched his idea, people worshipped idols and he was presenting oneness of Allah (SWT). His idea was completely against the ruling convention of the society. There were several idols installed inside the holy mosque and some were erected in the open places of Makkah. A few people were practicing the religion of Ibrahim (AS) who believed in the oneness of Allah (SWT). And Christian and Jews of the time were expecting a new prophet(ﷺ). Therefore, they had some soft corner for the prophet (ﷺ) and the new religion.

Politically, most of Arabs were independent and tribal system was in place. The absence of a united government was making exceedingly difficult for someone who wanted to unite them.

There was no intervention of government /tribal system on business activities. The absence of any law was making it difficult to plan something with certainty. Experts believe that laws govern business conditions and in turn, they impact on planning activities. Some of them are as follows:

- Education Law
- Anti-trust law
- Employment law
- Discrimination law
- Data protection law
- Environmental Law
- Health and safety law[5]

Consequently, the level of corruption was at the peak. The powerful were oppressing the weak,

---

[5] http://ecothunk.uk/PDF/Political%20Factors%20Affecting%20Business%20(13BS).pdf

slavery was common, tribal leaders were acting like uncrowned kings, daughters were buried live, women were in worst conditions, religious activities were ridiculous and so on.

Travel to Abyssinia

Assumptions about the social and political environment under which the plan would work or be carried out at the occasion of the above so-called migration were not very much different from the one described above. There were truly slight changes in the overall social and political conditions. However, the security was getting tight. A range of developments took place so far. Muslims used to pray slat outside the city in the open air. One day many infidels spotted them and made ridicule of them; Saad (RA) wounded one of them. It begins the struggle, armed one but Allah, the exalted, revealed to His prophet (ﷺ) that the time is for patience and restrain.

Two delegates of Quraysh approached Abu Talib to restrain his nephew for preaching the new religion. The prophet (ﷺ) said in response to the demand of the second delegate that, "if they put the sun in my right hand and the moon in my left hand, I would never stop it" because he was deputed for it. Quraysh could not harm the prophet (ﷺ) due to the respect of Abu Talib, but they did not spare his noble companions especially those who were poor and weak.

Meanwhile, Abuzer of Ghaffar (RA) clan and Tofyl (RA) of Daws clan who were living in the outstrips of Makkah took the profession of faith. They started to work upon their clans and slowly and steadily increased clan men/women joined their hands. The rays of light also lit the neighbourhood of Yasrib, an area of Jews and two polytheist tribes: Aows and Khizrij. Both Jews and these tribes were waiting for a prophet (ﷺ) to come from the South. A delegate of Aows travelled to Makkah to buy the alliance of Quraysh against their arch rival Khizrij. They could not motivate the potential ally but heard about the prophet (ﷺ). The prophet (ﷺ) always was in pursuit of any opportunity for conveying his message, found them. One of them was in favour of the message but other kept themselves deprived of the bounty of Allah, the exalted. And returned to the home.

Meanwhile, Hamzah (RA) professed the faith of Islam; Abu Jahl teased the prophet (ﷺ) while Hamza (RA) was out of the city. On his way-back, he was informed about the mishap. He struck his arrow holder on his head, but Abu Jahl did not dare to retaliate. This type of small episodes of oppression was a matter of daily activity. Quraysh was disturbed and wanted to find a way out. They used to hold meetings of their leaders; during such a meeting, they thought Muhammad (ﷺ) would be doing all that for a purpose. So, let us offer him what might be the reasons for the preaching. The sent a delegate to him to offer him three alternatives: if you are doing all this to gain power, we could accept you our king, if you wanted to become a rich person, we can gather a lot of richness for you, and you would be the richest among us. However, if you did not feel well, we can find out an expert who can treat your ailment. The plan of migration was made under these circumstances.

Treaty of Mina

Several events appeared from the movement of Abyssinia. Two delegates approached Abu Talib for seizing the preaching. He tried to convince the prophet (ﷺ) but how he could stop a job for which he was deputed. And it was the eternal life-saving prescription for humanity for the foolish demands of those who were chronic patients of the most fatal disease of the world, shirk. It is like a patient who needs an operation to transplant his organ to save his life. The doctor tries to remove his non-functional parts of his body and he objects. Some time he abuses verbally or physically. The infidels were trying to eliminate the prophet (ﷺ) in the same manner. They made many attempts for it but failed.

Meanwhile, Islam of Hamzah (RA) and Umer (RA) forced them to restrain because they were famous for bravery and strength. Despite these developments, the opponents made efforts to martyr the prophet (ﷺ). Abu Talib was feeling the heat, he thought the danger may be subsidised provided a tribal card was used. People used to support any thing for the name of their tribe no matter whether the involved person (s) was right or wrong. Abu Talib and most of his clan men were not considering the prophet (ﷺ) right but could stand behind him for tribal honour. Abu Talib knew the fact; therefore, he called a meeting of two branches of Abd-e-Manaaf: Banu Hashim and Banu Mutalib. Put a suggestion about the protection of the prophet (ﷺ) due to the nature of the potential danger. They accepted it except Abu Lahab.

When other clans realised it, they also planned to retaliate. They devised a novel tactic, social and economic boycott with above mentioned clans. It continued for three years which was a bundle of inhuman activities. Children were suffering, women dried out their breasts in hunger to produce few drops of milk for their loved ones. Common people forced to eat dry leaves; it was a common to sacrifice for Banu Hashim and Mutalib, but they never gave up. At last Allah, the exalted, recued them and the blocked ended.

The tests were following each other. The prophet (ﷺ) said to the nearest effect, I have been tested the most among prophets (AS) because he was dearer to his Lord. When he was honoured with the prophethood, he said the tests have started. At the death bed he said, this was the last day of his tests, his agonies. Soon after the end of the boycott his material patron and the tribal umbrella flew away, Abu Talib made his way to the eternity. And even more shocking, his beloved wife and internal pillar of the home also left him for good. Khadija (RA), the mother of Muslims and a staunch supporter, motivator, and benefactor disappeared.

However, the ray of hope emerged from the North. People of Madinah started to enter Islam. Six in the first year, twelve in the following year. The took the oath of obedience and became the backdrop of the famous treaty of Mina, commonly known as *Biat Uqba Sania*. More than seventy Yasrabi men invited him to join them in the new land.

Hijrah expedition

Iqbal and Ahmad (2009) put the assumption of the prophet (ﷺ) in the following words in connection with the Hijrah expedition,

> The Prophet (peace be on him)'s assumptions were based on the premise that the external environment was extremely hostile to the plan especially the security situation was so risky that the migrants could lose their lives during the implementation process. The Prophet (peace be on him) had a firm belief in the success of the plan. He handed over all the "safe keepings" of the people to 'Ali and

advised him to return them to their owners and then reach to Yathrib. He also encouraged Abu Bakr in the cave when he was worried about the possibility of entrance of enemy inside the cave; "do not worry Allah is with us."[6]

The opposition was at the peak at when the prophet (ﷺ) had to leave his sweat home. The last peg was planned but the enemy could not make it. Most of the Muslims already took their way to the new land. The prophet (ﷺ) was waiting for the Divine commandment. It arrived. The prophet (ﷺ) asked Abu Bakker (RA) to get prepared and accompany him; the noble team headed towards the new destination and Islam took a new turn for prosperity.

---

[6] P. 60.

Integration

Migration was the beginning of a new era where issues took a distinct perspective than those of Makkah. Social and economic factors emerged compared to security and religious matters. Molana Mubarikpuri (1995)[7] states that there were three communities in Madinah. The first one was Muslims. Among them, migrants were nowhere economically because they barely saved their lives to reach Madinah. One of the companions paid all his wealth including two maids to buy his life. Abu Salma (RA) had to leave his wife and the only son to get rid of the enemy. The lion of Islam like Umer (RA) could not bring anything. Abu Bakker (RA) had left his entire family behind.

The migrants needed economic support and social integration. Although they were a community themselves because they were dwellers of Makkah and most of them were relatives yet they were living as guests. A guest

---

[7] Mubarikpuri (1995)

cannot feel comfortable for a long time; he does not enjoy privacy and sweetness of his own home. The Helpers were economically well off and wanted to help their migrant brothers in Islam, a new relationship that never existed. They needed social integration. It suggests that a new culture had to create. Both were also different in nature. The migrants were traders, and the Helpers were formers who own agricultural land and gardens. Their marriage could produce a new community with a blend of the culture of Makkah and Madinah.

Muslims were a new community itself which needed integration with Jews and other idolaters of the area. The prophet (ﷺ) started from Muslims. He has created the system of brotherhood. The responsibility was evenly distributed; one person of migrants was made a brother of one person of Madinah. The prophet (ﷺ) did it carefully, knowledgeable migrant became a brother of the same nature. A leader or his son was handed over to a leader of

Madinah. Thus, the prophet (ﷺ) kept the social status in mind while making the pairs.

The idolaters were of two kinds: some were simple people, and they supported the new government. Others were secret followers of Abdullah bin Abi who was an undeclared leader of the big tribes: Aows and Khizraj. After the war of Baas, both tribes principally agreed upon his leadership, but the formal announcement was not yet made. The arrival of the prophet (ﷺ) faded away all his hopes. So, he played the role of Abu Jehl in Madinah but as a hypocrite because open opposition was not possible for him or his followers.

The third group was the Jewish community. They were influential economically and socially. According to their books, a new prophet (ﷺ) was about to come; they recognised the prophet, but irony of fate impedes their way to enjoy the mercy of the prophet (ﷺ). Despite their hostility the prophet (ﷺ) had made a peace treaty with them. The purpose was to remove the barriers between the communities to understand each other.

These measures stabilised the political and security environment in and around Madinah. The prophet (ﷺ) had also done similar truce with other tribes so expand the scope of the government and to create the influence of Muslims.

Treaty with Jews

Since the political situation was not in favour of Muslims in Madinah therefore, some measures were necessary to stabilise them. Jews were a significant power, so a treaty was required to strengthen the situation. The prophet (ﷺ) assumed several factors to initiate the dialogue for the purpose. For example, Jews were not idols worshippers and were holders of the Book. So, there was a common ground and the shared values with them. They were strong in military terms because they had constructed castles and other military facilities. He also assumed that the Helpers were weak especially after the recent war between them. Muslims were not strong enough apparently; they needed some cushion. They required time to establish themselves. In addition, there was a time to clarify the relations between the parties. And there should be some reference to determine the scope of these relations which would provide a structure for them. The treaty with Jews was signed to entertain these issues.

It suggests that a lenient policy was required. Therefore, the prophet (ﷺ) had offered them some favourable terms albeit they were not against the fundamentals of Islam. For instance, blood money etc shall be the same as it was prevalent. Jews shall enjoy religious freedom and relationship between the parties shall be friendly.

Treaty of Hodabia

He assumed at Hodabia that a peace treaty would provide opportunities to develop social relations with Quraysh who were unaware about the Islamic way of life. It would enable them to understand and consider Islam. As a result, people of Makkah used to visit Madinah to their relatives. They observed their life style. Abu Sufyan once visited one of the wives of the prophet (ﷺ) who was his daughter and realised the respect and love of his daughter for the prophet (ﷺ). When Quraysh breached the pact, he visited respected companions to talk about the revival of the treaty. Although he could not receive any gesture of revival yet because of the treaty he peacefully visited Madinah and approached the desired people.

Secondly, Muslim believed that they could delay concentrating on other Arab tribes. The time witnessed that many people embraced Islam during the period i.e. from the treaty to the conquered of Makkah. There were 1400 soldiers at the Hodabia which increased to 10,000 in two years' time at the fall of Makkah to the Muslims.

The third assumption was creating political stability. A stable system of government was established during the period. The basic structure was put into action. Peace truces were either made or the existing were strengthened. Jews were treated both in political terms and in military dimensions.

The war of Badr

Several developments took place after the above measures which were the back drop of the armed event. Quraysh tried to seduce hypocrite of Madinah to expel Muslims out of Madinah or wage a war against them. They wrote a letter to the implied head of infidels of Madinah which emphasis for a battle against Muslims. The prophet (ﷺ) initiated dialogue with hypocrites and warmed them for the consequences. Consequently, they refrained from their intentions.

Quraysh also threatened migrants and Helpers separately regarding their intentions. They warned migrants that you are not out of our reach though you managed to escape. The prophet (ﷺ) was worried about his own safety;

he established a security plan for him. A team was looking after him all the time. Later, Allah, the exalted, revealed to him that the Divine protection was provided to him.

Saad bin Maaz (RA) went for Umrah where Abu Jehl warned him that you have harbour our people, but we reserve the right to take "corrective action". Had he not with Umya bin Khalf (his host), he would not go back to Madinah. Saad (RA) replied, yes if you would stop us from Umrah we would black your way to Syria, the trade route of Makkah.

The threat of blockage of trade rout was a serious matter for them. The prophet (ﷺ) knew it; thus, he devised a plan to make it unsafe and to extend the political influence in and around the trade rout. He had included more tribes in the alliance especially those who were residing along with the trade route. It was in the response to their threat to migrants and Helpers. And terrifying idolaters of Madinah to wage a war against Muslims. As a pre-emptive strike, he also sent or lead some small expeditions to send a strong message to Quraysh that their hostilities were noticed in Madinah. These expeditions became the preface of the war of Badr.

Makkah under the flag of Islam

The prophet had assumed several factors to initiate the campaign. The beginning point was the sending of an envoy to Quraysh about the treaty of Hodabia. The first two conditions conveyed to them were difficult for them to fulfil. Quraysh was not paying the blood money to Khaza, the effected tribe. They would also not separate themselves of their confederates, Banu Amir. It was against their tribal honour. Hence, they abruptly accepted the third condition but that was an emotional decision. They realised it soon, but the bullet left the chamber.

Under the guidance of Almighty, the prophet (ﷺ) wanted to take a decisive step. He did not entertain the post cancellation struggle of

Quraysh to restore the treaty. He assumed that it was the right time to hit the warm iron. Consequently, the time has come when dreams come true. The prophet (ﷺ) had kept the mission secret so that Quraysh could not get prepared for an encounter. They must be caught suddenly. His purpose was to avoid bloodshed. Therefore, the mission was kept so secret that even the ally tribes did not leak the intentions of Muslims.

Miscellaneous

War of trench: Previous two arm encounters did not produce a favourable result for Quraysh. They assumed that it was due to lack of material resources, albeit Allah, the exalted, had made the decisions but it was beyond their comprehension. Therefore, they thought more resources could do the job. They seduced and gathered almost entire Arab army to initiate a decisive invasion. Their number of troops were 10,000 or so. Muslims army was only 3,000. It was a heavy odd in terms of numbers but previous "war games" were almost fought with a similar ratio.

The prophet (ﷺ) assumed that it was a practical idea to leave the residential area and defend themselves outside the city. The city was encircled three sides with gardens and constructed neighbourhood while one side was open. It required defence. It helped Muslims to separate women and children from the heat of the war.

Another issue was many opposing forces who were equipped with iron from head to toe. The prophet (ﷺ) assumed that the war must be staged outside the city to keep vulnerable people separate.

5 Determining alternatives

In this phase, various alternatives were considered. According to Knootz and Weihrich (2006), "the fourth step in planning is to search and examine alternative courses of action, especially those not immediately apparent." Given that let us examine various instances regarding the matter.

Movement to Abyssinia

There were certain issues to consider Abyssinia as an alternative destination. The first issue was to *protect the followers*. The opposition was getting stern. Muslims were living under sever circumstances: oppression, fear, and hatred. Albeit the number of Muslims crossed the triple figure in the 5th year of the prophet (ﷺ) but overall environment of Makkah was tense, soft hearted people like Usman bin Affan (RA) were also feeling the heat. It was the demand of the time to think about the small but growing team of followers.

The second was to practice Islam freely and peacefully. The king of Abyssinia was a soft-hearted person and believed to be a practicing, Christian. Muslims could *practice Islam* freely in the new country because the king of the country was a just ruler. The prophet (ﷺ) wanted to *export the idea*, his product. It was the right time to take a bold decision.

The prophet (ﷺ) formed a team of 15/16 individuals under the leadership of Usman (RA). The high-profile team he has selected shows his intention. It included famous companions like Abdul Rahman bin Aof (RA), Zubair bin Awwaam (RA), Masab bin Omair (RA), Abu Salma (RA), Abu Huzaifa (RA), Abdullah bin Masood (RA), and Abu Hatab bin Umro (RA). Women include the daughter of the prophet (ﷺ), Usman (RA)'s wife and Um-e-Salma who became the wife of the prophet (ﷺ) later. They supposed to convey the message of Allah (SWT); it was one of the major objectives of the expedition.

When the prophet (ﷺ) received the good news that the team was doing well and practically demonstrating Islam to the inhibitors of the country, he despatched another bigger team of 103 members under the leadership of Jaffer bin Abi Talib (RA). The team had enjoyed the opportunity to present Islam in the court of the king of Habshah. It created a positive impact on the minds of the king who later took shelter under the fold of Islam.

Journey of Taif

Taif journey was made at the peak of opposition because Quraysh increased their mean activities after the death of Abu Talib in the year 10 of Nabvi. There were a couple of options available to continue the journey of success: to continue the effort in Makkah or to take it to nearby areas where it could flourish. The prophet (ﷺ) was already in search of an alternative place to establish the new base camp; he tried to do so in

Abyssinia but could not find a reasonable response. Therefore, Taif was a lucrative alternative.

There were two alternatives to initiate the journey: to make it secretly or openly. The prophet (ﷺ) opted the former. He did not take a camel to keep it secret. He usually takes Abu Bakker (RA) for such initiative but he wanted to keep it top secret. Taking Abu Bakker (RA) could be noticed in Makkah because the population was small and key figures like Abu Bakker (RA) could be spotted. It was also possible that Quraysh could impede the journey. The prophet (ﷺ) took his slave who was also his adopted son with him. The team walked away from about 70 km. It could be the longest walking journey in his life.

Conquer of Makkah

Since Quraysh helped Banu Bakker for killing the confederate clan of Muslims (Banu Khaza) therefore, Banu Khaza approached the prophet (ﷺ) for help. He put forward three conditions

Quraysh for the resolution of the issue. They were:

1. Pay the ransom of Khaza.
2. Discontinue your support to Banu Bakker (so that Muslims could deal with them directly)
3. The truce of Hodabia would no more effective according to which there was peace between the parties.

Quraysh opted the last one. Thus, Muslims had no option but to act against Quraysh and their confederate Banu Bakker. Later, Quraysh realised the gravity of the situation and their blunder for selecting the third option and tried to restore the treaty of Hodabia. But the prophet (ﷺ) had decided to make a decisive decision to teach a lesson to Quraysh for good.

The prisoners of war of Badr

The prisoners of war also generated options for him. Two options emerged as an outcome of consultation with the companions:

1-To handover each prisoner to his relative who should kill him.

2-To set them free for the blood money or ransom.

He could put them under sward with a single gesture, but he opted the soft approach. And it was justifiable because these were the people who did not allow him to call towards one Allah, the exalted two years ago. They were the one who encircled his home with naked swards to get rid of him for ever. The example is enough for those who hold the view that Islam was spread with sward. The prophet (ﷺ) offered the prisoners to pat ransom and get free.

A softer option was adopted for those who could not pay their freedom money. They were offered to teach ten illiterate persons and get themselves free.

Battle of Uhad

Now of Uhad, he consulted his colleagues about the viable options of places where defence line could be drawn. It could be possible to stay in Madinah or step out at an appropriate place to defend themselves. The prophet (ﷺ) selected the opinion of his colleagues and went out of the city to encounter the invasion.

The prophet (ﷺ) had defined a strategic move. Quraysh could not capitalise the upper hand gained in the battle of Uhad. They were not sure about their advantage and left the ground of battle quickly due to the fear of another episode. However, they realised on the way back to complete the win. Some of them wanted to reattack but could not dare to make it. The prophet (ﷺ) came to know their intentions, therefore, assembled the troops once again and marched towards enemy forces but the opponents could not dare to face the Muslim army. It changed the perception of the outcome. He could opt to stay in Madinah to wait for the enemy but his proactive approach turned the tables, and he went out of the city to draw the defence line.

Banu Nazeer

Banu Nazeer was a Jewish tribe in Madinah who was making lots of trouble. For example, he did not pay the blood money due to him regarding the murder of two members of Banu Amir. When the prophet (ﷺ) tried to resolve the matter, their people tried to harm him. The prophet's (ﷺ) strategy was to address the issue with peaceful means, but Banu Nazeer was deceiving. Consequently, the prophet (ﷺ) decided to deal with them with heavy hands. They were also offered to renew a previous truce, but they refused. It compelled the prophet (ﷺ) to take military action which was the feasible option. He adopted the option as a last resort to resolve the matter. We can say that the prophet (ﷺ) had determined two alternatives:

1. Resolution of the matter peacefully
2. Go for a military action.

The opponents did not accept the first one thus the second option has opted.

6 Comparing alternatives courses

According to the authors of the planning model it "involves examining weak and strong points of each alternative and weighing them in light of *premises and goals.*" There is a trade-off between what is available and what is not. Good planners weighed them to select the best one. The prophet (ﷺ) encountered similar situations. Few examples would clarify it. And the parameters he applied for the selection of a particular one.

The Hijrah

One of the major projects was the Hijrah from Makkah. Since the security situation was serious, therefore, he had to select timings, the route, and the strategy of leaving.

For instance, let us look at the timing of his journey. He left his home middle of the night. He could leave in the early hours of the night but people could spot him. There was enough time from midnight to the dawn to reach the first destination. If he would choose to leave his home in the late hours of the night, the worriers could attack him as they had planned. It could also have made difficult for the team to reach the cave safely. According to Iqbal and Ahmad (2009) about travelling from Makkah to Madinah, "The Prophet (peace be on him) had two possible alternatives: (i) leave Makkah and travel towards Yathrib straight away and (ii) leave the city and stay at a nearby destination or hiding place, wait until a possible search dies out, and then start the journey towards Yathrib."[8]

In general, the alternative to Hijrah was to stay in Makkah. It was not safe to stay anymore. The plan was already made to eliminate him. His home was already under siege. The best alternative was to leave the city. Another possibility could leave his own home and stay with one of his

---

[8] P. 61.

relatives, but the warriors could reach there. If the opponents try to capture him, the prophet's (ﷺ) clan would not allow them which could start afresh war. His Hijrah resolved all these issues for ever. And achieved all the envisioned objectives. For instance, the objectives of Hijrah were as described above were,

> The objective of the hajrah was to spread Islam freely in the new land. Makkans were unable to stop him or his companions to do so. Muslims were also safe of their hostility. The prophet (ﷺ) established the first Islamic state in Madinah which was the ultimate objective of his life so that organised efforts should be made for the success of his mission.

The other journey of Hijrah achieved all the objectives as envisioned in the original plan.

The battle of Uhad

At the time of Uhad the prophet (ﷺ) identified two alternatives: stay in the city and defend and go out to find an appropriate place for the event. He has opted the later alternative with the consultation of his team. The first option was a defensive strategy but the safety of vulnerable people like women and children were at risk. The second option resolved the issue, and the subsequent events showed the decision was correct.

Abyssinia

When the prophet considered the options for migration of his companions to a foreign country. He had considered the circumstances in Makkah and in Abyssinia. He made a comparison based on objectives he had articulated for the purpose. Remember his objectives were:

• Safety of his companions

• Free practice of Islam in the new place

• Propagation of Islam in the new land

These objectives were defined due to the deteriorating security situation in Makkah. Muslims were few and were poor people of the community or of incredibly soft nature such as Abu Bakker and Usman bin Affan (RA). By that time Muslims were not able to practice Islam freely and openly. There was a pressing need of the time to export the idea. The prophet (ﷺ) also wanted to shift his base camp from Makkah to somewhere where it could flourish. The king of Abyssinia was famous for his justice. He was also a practicing Christian; Christian had many things common with Islam such as they were followers of a Heavenly book. So, Abyssinia was a strong candidate which could promise the objectives.

Hodabia

With the command of Allah (SWT), the prophet (ﷺ) instructed to prepare for Umrah. But Quraysh was determined to stop Muslims from fulfilling the command of Allah, the exalted. Muslims were wearing the special dress for the purpose, and they had marked the animals for sacrifice to show everyone that they were heading Makkah for the ritual.

Quraysh sent a cavalry of 200 horse riders under the command of Khalid bin Waleed. He was waiting for Muslim caravan on the famous track, but the prophet (ﷺ) had changed his way to avoid an armed encounter.

It suggests that the prophet (ﷺ) had two alternatives: war or peace. In case of war, there was a chance of human loss. The Muslim even after winning the war would go back or could do Umrah. But the peace option gave them plenty of time to establish themselves. They did it during the next two years of peace. Their main purpose was to spread Islam which reached more people of Arab lands.

He had opted peace despite companions were ready for war. Secondly, he wanted to abstain from war for the larger interest of Muslims. He delayed through the treaty which enhanced his efforts. Two years later when he engaged with war to the same party, the number of troops alone were seven times more than the number he accompanied at the time of the treaty. The enemy was helpless to defend himself because of a better strategy of the prophet (ﷺ). His strategy was a success as the subsequent events showed.

Integration

The scale of migration that took place in the name of Allah, the exalted, was unprecedented but the next key questions were how the migrants could be settled. One option was to establish a separate camp for them where they could enjoy their privacy, regional intimacy, and tribal harmony. But Islam does not believe in these factors. For Islam, all human being are the children of Adham (AS) who was created from dust. They are equal; no one is superior because of race, region, material possession or colour.

If look at the situation, migrants could say they are superior because they are from the tribe of the prophet (ﷺ), they are the one who supported the prophet (ﷺ) first, they are the one who left their homes for the sake of Islam and so on. The Helpers could say we embraced Islam while we were not of his city, his tribe, we invited him to our home land, and we have assumed the opposition of entire Arab land for him. We have provided him with safety, peace, and shelter. We are well off and so on. But the prophet (ﷺ) eliminated all these factors of reference and said, Arab has no superiority over non-Arab, and white is no more superior to black. The honour belongs to fear of Allah, the exalted only.

He had three options to deal with the situation. Leave the migrants to manage themselves, establish a separate camp for them and integrate both as brothers. The Helpers already gave an oath to the prophet (ﷺ) in Mina that they would protect him as they do to their children and wives. Therefore, implementation of the third option seemed viable.

7 Choosing the most promising one.

When we examine the selection of the prophet (ﷺ); it looks amazing. The right selection is linked with the outcome. There was hardly any selection which did not produce the positive results. Let us investigate some of these.

Integration

The biggest challenge after Hijrah was to integrate two distinct cultures. The migrants and Helpers. The prophet (ﷺ) did it successfully. As we have seen in the previous chapter that there were three options available to the prophet (ﷺ). He has selected to integrate both the communities. In terms of results, it was interesting to note that the pair of Helpers and Migrants lived and shared resources happily.

There was no single instance of any misunderstanding or quarrel among them.

He developed brotherhood according to the social and economic status of the parties concerned. Abdurrahman bin Aouf become the brother of (the wealthiest person of Madinah), Saad bin Al-Rabi. Saeed bin Zaid (RA) was among the ten who honoured with glad tiding of paradise in this world was a knowledgeable person became the brother of another such an intellectual, Abi bin Kaab (RA) who was the writer of revelation and the leader of the "Reader of Quran" i.e. *quara*. Abu Huzaifah (RA) was the son of Utba bin Rabia, a leader of the Quraysh became the brother of the leader of a clan called Ashal. Abu Ubaidah Al-Jarrah (RA) was honoured with the title of "Ameen al-Ummah" (Trustworthy of the Nation) became the brother of the leader of the clan called Aows, Saad bin Maaz (RA). The former conquered Syria later.

Taif journey

As we understand that the prophet (ﷺ) was in search of a place where activities of the movement might be shifted. He sent two delegations to Abyssinia but there was no progress in this regard. There were a couple of reasons which induce him to consider Taif as an alternative. The other option was to continue efforts of propagation in Makkah but it reached its upper limit. The prophet (ﷺ) had squeezed the city but there were no signs of any goodness. It means there was no improvement. As an expert planner and administrator, he wanted to progress. Later, he said to the nearest effect that one is today should be better than his yesterday. Keeping it in mind, he intended to travel to the new city.

He was injured and cruelly treated in Taif; the angels were on his command at the conclusion of the journey but he selected the most promising alternative. It created an impression on the human kind. The tribe accepted Islam later. One of them (Muhammad bin Qasim) took the message of the prophet (ﷺ) to the Indian subcontinent. There are more than 600 million Muslims residing in the area at the time of this writing. His journey to Taif produced all that which we feel and observe today. That was the outcome of his sacrifice and perseverance. He had opted it above emotional clouds. Thus, the rationality prevailed.

The war of Trench

There were two options to encounter the enemy. The first was to compete with traditional strategy as was done in the previous two episodes. The second was to invent a solution. The prophet (ﷺ) invented it. He decided to dig a trench between the competing forces. His selection was not only an innovative initiative but also caused to restrict the enemy to launch a full-fledged war. The enemy lost courage and supplies to continue to siege. Consequently, forced to uplift it.

The second example of his selection of the most promising alternative was at the occasion of the war of Uhad. The battle of Uhad was undecided; the opponents caused damaged to Muslims but left the battlefield without any decisive outcome. They realised on the way back and wanted to relaunch the attack but could not dare to do so. The prophet (ﷺ) made another big decision after receiving the news of intentions of Quraysh. He recollected his army and followed them, but Quraysh could not sustain. It suggests that he opted a better alternative; he could stay in Madinah to wait for the response. Nevertheless, he initiated the offensive which turned the upper hand of the enemy into a technical defeat. They could not dare to stand to defend themselves.

Tabuk

A similar alternative was selected at the expedition of Tabuk. There was news of aggregation of the king of Rome. The king of Rome wanted to invade the Muslim state, the prophet (ﷺ) took many mujahedeen and marched to Tabuk to encounter him. The enthusiasm of Muslims restricted him to dare to challenge them. Again, there were two alternatives available to the prophet (ﷺ): to stay in Madinah and wait. It could encourage the opponents to siege the city. It would be a defensive approach, but the prophet (ﷺ) preferred to adopt an offensive strategy. It discouraged Romans and others to think twice before initiating any military campaign.

Hodabia

As we know there were two alternatives emerged at Hodabia: war or peace. The prophet (ﷺ) had opted the option which was declared "an open victory". The alternative did not seem attractive in the first instance, but it produced far reaching impacts on the life of Muslims. It opened the door of failure for Quraysh, the competing force. The prophet (ﷺ) had once again allowed the opponents to enjoy his soft approach to deal with serious matters.

His objective was to avoid confrontation, establish peace and to achieve strategic goals. The unfolding of events showed that his choice was the best alternative that emerged out of the situation.

Characteristics of selection

The prophet (ﷺ) used to choose alternative keeping in mind several factors. He had selected the softer solution for the prisoners of war at the occasion of Badr. It was to release them through payment of random. The alternative option was to kill them. He also preferred peace instead of war. The Hodabia pact was a good example. In this regard, he did peace treaties with Jews and other tribes of Madinah.

His other distinctive strategy was to avoid bloodshed. He could kill hundreds during the conquered of Makkah but he did not do it. He has not taken revenge for his enemy. The prophet (ﷺ) was not attacking opponents during the night to minimise casualties. At the occasion of Khyber, he did so. He ordered Ali (RA) at this occasion that first invite the opponents towards peace/Islam. If they accept your message, it is better for you than red camels. Islamic teaching says deal with people softly in all occupations. It forced one non-Muslim scholar to say that the prophet (ﷺ) of Islam has humanized the war because he ordered not harm trees, animals, save crops and so on. There were many people around 9/10 which damaged Islam the most and were still hostile at the fall of Makkah. Therefore, were exempted from the general pardon but four of them asked for forgiveness and the prophet (ﷺ) granted them. They included the person who martyred the prophet's (ﷺ) beloved uncle, Hamza (RA).

8 Formulating the supporting Plans

According to Iqbal and Ahmad (2009), it includes,

> The proponents of this planning model state that it should include a plan for buying necessary equipment, material, hire and train workers etc. In business organizations, a plan may need an additional plant and machinery, delivery vans, computers or other electronic devices and a new type of raw material/components. Existing employees may need new skills to operate new equipment. Sometimes new employees may be hired to put the plan into operation. The additional supply of resources may be required to ensure the smooth flow of raw

material and components. Supporting plans are prepared for each of these elements.[9]

If we look at the strategy of the prophet (ﷺ) to implement the grand plan, spread the message of Allah, the exalted; he defined plans to collect resources for various military expeditions and to run the affairs of the state. The system of the donation was introduced in the first instance. Individual collections were made to finance the campaigns. Later, the system of Zakat was introduced. It also includes the collection of tax from non-Muslims, a tax on agricultural produces and minerals etc. The supporting plans were in place to manage them.

Hijrah to Abyssinia was also a supporting plan for the spread of Islam. Two groups of companions were sent to the country to protect them and ask them to spread the message of Allah (SWT).

---
[9] P.63.

The plan was a success which caused the conversion of the king of the country later.

Intelligence security plans were in place to support the secrecy of the grand plan or any contingency plan. The prophet (ﷺ) wanted to march towards Makkah secretly so that bloodshed could be avoided and catch the enemy suddenly. A companion sent a letter to his family members in Makkah before the event to warn them. The prophet (ﷺ) was informed through the Divine sources about it. He sent a team to obtain the letter. Thus, the main plan was intact.

Battles were not his area of concern, but he planned them well. He has appointed a special team of archers to safeguard one point of enemy attack. He deemed it especially important and appointed 50 archers for the job. Muslims got upper hand in the battle and the battalion left the point and joined others in obtaining booty. Keen enemy eyes found it empty and made a flank attack which put the Muslim army in trouble. It caused martyr of many valuable lives. However, the plan itself was important and was the part of the far-reaching strategy of the prophet (ﷺ).

In connection with Hijrah Iqbal and Ahmad (2009) summarised the supporting plans as,

> He used two camels (the delivery transport), six persons (five of them were volunteers and only one was hired) and a handful of food stuff to implement the plan. Abu Bakr (RA) arranged the animals on the instruction of the Prophet (peace be upon him) who bought one from him.

There were three supporting plans. First was to remove the foot prints of the team or any other person visiting them (e.g. the son of Abu Bakker (RA) for delivering information about the activities of Quraysh). A slave of Abu Bakker (RA) was there for grazing the herd of sheep. He supposed to drive the herd over the foot prints of Abdullah bin Abu Bakker (RA) to prevent any security personnel of Quraysh to identify the foot prints. The second plan to ensure the supply of food. According to Molana Shibli (2004)[10], the same herd was brought near to the cave for milking the animals which the noble team was drinking as food. It worked for three days. The third plan to gather and deliver information about the activities of Quraysh. Abdullah bin Abu Bakker (RA) did the job. He spent all nights with the noble team but used to visit the city daily to know what was happening in the circles of Quraysh. He used to return to the cave and describe the story to the prophet (ﷺ) and his father.

Supporting plans also include training of personnel (Knootz and Weihrich, 2006). A raised platform was constructed near the masjid Nabvi for those who want to learn Islam. They vary in number but sometimes reach up to 100.[11] The

---

[10] Nomani, Shibli, and Syed Sulaiman Nadvi (2004)

[11] Kandehvi, Zakarya, Fazail-e-Amaal

prophet (ﷺ) or the Islamic government principally financed them. The participants learned, preserved, practice and disseminate it to others. They were ambassadors of Islam.

The prophet (ﷺ) had a supporting plan for delivering information; he sent a person to tell the good news of the victory of Badr that Quraysh and their allies received heavy defeat in the battle. It was important because Jews and others spread the rumour of assassination of the prophet (ﷺ) in Madinah. Some Muslims were left in Madinah including Usman bin Affan (RA) to look after his wife and one of the beloved daughters of the prophet(ﷺ); the prophet (ﷺ) sent two delegates to deliver the good news of the victory to them. The delegates reached rejoicingly and happily delivered the good news of victory.

Since the intention of the prophet (ﷺ) was not to fight but circumstances lead him to adopt the way to defend himself. Some key figures, who remained in Madinah, set to welcome the prophet (ﷺ) and his companions on the way back from Badr; they congratulated him and his victorious army.

Since a major expedition could happen any time, therefore, precautionary measures were necessary to get prepared for it. The prophet (ﷺ) also wanted to engage Quraysh so that Muslims can concentrate on others for propagating their idea. Truce with Jews was part of it and later Hodabia treaty was also such an effort. Quraysh expelled Muslims from Makkah and captured their properties so they needed some dose to realise what wrong they have done.

Another supporting plan was the blockade of their trade route which was their requirement and a weak point. To do this, the prophet (ﷺ) had according to Molana Mubarakpuri (1995) devised two supporting plans. First to make peace treaties with tribes who were living near or around the trade route. Second to guard the route physically through armed petrol. The later also included small encounters with those who resist.

While he was heading towards Hodabia, he consulted his colleagues about what to do. Two options emerged: first to avoid the possible encounter and the second if worse comes to worse, a war had to fight, Muslim would defend themselves with full force. Thus, the prophet (ﷺ) made the supporting plan to carry on the expedition. The companions were ready to face any potential odd. It was augmented when the oath was taken for a full-fledged war. Because the rumour was spread about the martyrdom of Muslim envoy, Usman bin Affan (RA). The oath was itself a contingency supporting plan. But we know the journey ended at the peace treaty.

At the occasion of Uhad supporting plan was articulated through the appointment of a small group of 50 archers because there was a chance of enemy attack from the pass. The battalion could also keep an eye on the movement of opposition troops. It was so important that Muslims were getting upper hand, and the enemy was leaving the battle ground, but the battalion left the pass. The enemy noticed the unguarded attacking point while the enemy company oversaw Khalid bin Waleed, a well-known military commander. He made a flunk attack and Muslims suffered heavy loss.

9 Quantifying Plans

It is helpful to qualify the resources used or to be applied in a plan or supporting plans. According to the proponents of the model capital expenditure need quantification so that available resources may be matched with requirements. It helps planners to arrange additional resources and employ them carefully. The model emphasises quantification of capital expenditure which are the resources through which more resources are produced. They also help to implement a plan e.g. camels in a journey. They are the fundamentals of any activity. For example, plant and machinery, transport vehicles etc.

The prophet (ﷺ) always decided of them. For instance, on Hijrah, there were two she-camels for transportation. The prophet (ﷺ) had bought one for himself while Abu Bakker (RA) had his own. A special guide was employed to show the track to the destination. A volunteer officer (Abdullah bin Abu Bakker (RA)) was doing the job of an information officer. Another person was providing food; he was also looking after the herd of sheep. It was used for food and removing footsteps of the information official who was visiting the travellers on daily basis. He was commuting to the city to gather information.

Although there was no department of finance at the beginning of the new state but established later. Required resources used to be collected just before the initiation of a project. The state was responsible for the provision of resources in war time. The largest number of troops were accompanied at the occasion of Tabuk. The estimate was around 30, 000. Usman bin Affan (RA) financed the battalion partly. The rest of the resources were collected prior to the expedition. It includes means of transport, food, and arms. Guides, paramedics, internal security etc personnel used to be the part of all expeditions.

There was an arrangement for recording the details of participants in a note book. It was the database of the time. For example, there was 313 personnel in Badr, 700 in Uhad, 1,400 in Hodabia, 3,000 in Khandaq, 10,000 in the expedition of Makkah and 12, 000 in Honain. It suggests that corresponding resources were arranged accordingly.

The prophet (ﷺ) used to judge the number of personnel required for a project. He sent a group of 70 for a job, 300 for another task and 3000 accompanied Zaid bin Harsa (RA), the team that set out after passing away of the prophet (ﷺ).

Quantification was also important to deal with the *spoils of war*. The companions used to collect it randomly at the end or during combat. They were distributed equally among the participants. The first job was to count it according to distinct categories such as camels, sheep, arms, and other items. And then to distribute them on an equal basis. At least basic mathematics was applied.

The prophet (ﷺ) was allocating human resources in a systematic way. He appointed a supervisor upon ten persons and advised to elect a leader when three persons are involved to do something. It is known as span of control in modern management terms. Many personnel were managed in the same way on separate occasions of wars. More than 124,000 at the final hajj.

He has divided the work in the chunks and responsibility was assigned to them i.e. employed the resources. Molana Shibli states that at the occasion of the war of trench, the prophet (ﷺ) had demarcated the boundaries of the trench and ten persons were assigned 10 yards for digging it. It took 3,000 soldiers twenty days to complete the job. So, the prophet (ﷺ) had estimated the amount of work and then divided it according to the manpower available.

The ghazwa Honain took place following the conquered of Makkah. The enemy was strong and there were new Muslims in the army who joined the Islamic troops after the big event. It pressurised the resources. Therefore, the prophet had borrowed 30, 000 dirhams and 100 shields and their accessories (Nomani and Nadvi, 1995). The resources were used to finance the campaign and equip the troops.

Resources used to be collected for various projects and the projects brought a lot of return as well. There were 6000 prisoners of war who could be the source of more finance in terms of the ransom their relatives might pay to free them. According to the rules of the time, the prisoners of war become slaves if their guardians did not pay the ransom. But the prophet (ﷺ) and his companions set them free for the pleasure of Allah, the exalted.

In addition, there were 24, 000 camels, more than 40, 000 small animals and 4,000 oqia silver. All were distributed except 1/5 which according to sharia belonged to the state. It is known as khams which is the share of needy people and the expenditures of the Islamic government.

The prophet (ﷺ) had bestowed 1,300 camels upon the new Muslims to win over their heart. Abu Sufyan (RA) and his family were given 120 Oqia and 300 camels. Some were granted 50 camels. Each soldier received 4 camels and 40 goats while horse riders were entitled three times more than a normal soldier. (Nomani and Nadvi 1995).

Following the truce of Hodabia where Allah (SWT) promised good news and a lot of material resources, the time had come for its emergence. Jews of Khyber were strong in number and wealth. The prophet (ﷺ) had decided to deal with them because they were involved in the recent battle and articulated conspiracy against Muslims.

There were many castles in the area spread over two parts. Since hypocrites did not participate in the previous battle, therefore, they were not allowed to take part in it. All the companions of Hodabia truce was taken to Khyber; we know they were 1400. Among them, 200 were horse riders. The troops were not ready for a battle in the Umrah campaign, but the army was fully equipped with military hardware on this occasion. The castles fell to Muslims one after another; some with fight and others peacefully. The prophet's (ﷺ) strategy was to minimise human loss. He advised Ali (RA) as a commander of one of the toughest tasks that first invite opponents towards Islam. If the enemy did not accept it than raise your sword because if a single person would receive guidance i.e. Islam, then it better for you more than red camels, the desired property. The prophet (ﷺ) also did not attack enemy in the dark of night so that enemy can think before initiating any military campaign. On one occasion Jews requested for a peace dialogue, the prophet (ﷺ) accepted their offer. Consequently, a peace pact was agreed upon according to which the Jews had to leave the area and they can take some gears with them. Later, they requested to stay in their homes but would pay half of the production of the cultivated lands. The prophet (ﷺ) accepted it.

Anyway, the end game was won with the nominal loss.; Muslims martyr was 18 or 19 and Jews lost 93 people according to Molana Mubarikpuri (1995).

The entire property obtained from the campaign was huge. There were 1400 troops including 200 horse riders; the property was divided into two parts: half to the state and another half for the army. For convenience, it was decided into 3 600 equal parts. Of them, 1800 for the government i.e. for the poor or any other contingency requirement. The other half was divided into 1800 portions. Each soldier would receive one portion and each horse rider would receive three times (two portions for the horse and one for the rider). The prophet (ﷺ) had received as a normal soldier.

We have described the spoils of war which in contemporary management is equivalent to the bonuses or any other payment made to the employee due to superior performance and bumper profits. Similarly, when management implements a new change programme like Total Quality Management or Business Process Management to enhance performance; they reward those who are involved in such an initiative. Therefore, it is a part of the plan for how the employees would be rewarded. As we understand that the prophet (ﷺ) used to finance the projects through contribution. Since at times everyone used to own the weapons required as part of self-defence thus armour was not required. However, some weapons were lost or broke during the combat which needed replenishing. There must be some reserve stock to satisfy the needs as well. It suggests that the management of spoils of war were necessary to implement future.

10 Implications for Managers

In addition to the application of the model offered, several learning aspects stem from the above discussion. They are taken in turn in the following paragraphs.

Planning characteristics
Looking at the entire strategy of the prophet (ﷺ) reveals a couple of learning points other than the model we have used as a reference to analyse the case. Let us examine them to know the meaning between the lines.

The prophet (ﷺ) had defined a grand plan and its associated objectives. It was to convey the message of Allah, the exalted to mankind. In the last sermon, he asked his companions about it. He said whether he had conveyed the message of his Creator, they replied, yes, the prophet (ﷺ)

of Allah (SWT). You have done to the best of your capacity.

He has made alternative plans assuming optimistic and pessimistic scenarios. For example, when he was travelling for Umrah, the enemy was trying to stop him. Before Hodabia, he made two plans. First was to avoid an armed encounter. For it, he was travelling on the unusual route while the opponents were coming from the normal trade route. Another plan was to get mentally ready to defend themselves if they were forced to fight. It was a contingency plan.

The prophet (ﷺ) had also articulated and implemented supporting plans. Technically, migration to Abyssinia, a journey of Taif, treaty of Mina etc were supporting plans.

In addition, the prophet (ﷺ) had also articulated contingency plans as he did before Hodabia truce.

The prophet's (ﷺ) plans were innovative. He stayed in the cave for three days during Hijrah. He travelled on a different path during the same expedition. He dug a trench as a defence shield for the third armed encounter.

He has divided the grand plan into small parts to deal with a particular aspect of the plan like intelligence management, finance, and supplies.

Management approach

The ingredients of the prophet's (ﷺ) management strategy included a couple of characteristics. He used to opt a lenient alternative. He adopted the softer view of Abu Bakker (RA) at the occasion of prisoners of war of Badr. Second, he was always consulting his colleagues. He has consulted at the occasion of war of Trench, Badr, before Hodabia treaty etc.

He has utilised resources prudently; he had allocated 10 yards of the peace of the trench to a group of ten personnel. He took full benefit of the enormous number of troops at the occasion of conquering of Makkah to avoid bloodshed. The power was demonstrated to the than leader of Quraysh to impress him so that he could estimate the strength of Muslims and their resources to think about to compete with the army.

The prophet (ﷺ) had applied a structured approach to achieve his objectives. As soon as he arrived in Madinah, he created brotherhood among Muslims and signed a peace treaty with Jews, a significant political and military power. When he started armed expeditions on and around trade route of Makkah, he signed peace pacts with the tribes living in the area. Thus, ensure the stability of the route before initiating the military campaign. The prophet (ﷺ) also ensured every aspect of security prior to migration. The details about it were decided in the truce of Mina. While advanced towards Makkah, Quraysh was kept unaware of the military efforts. It was one of the best examples of intelligence management despite all allied tribes were informed about the intentions of Muslims. There was complete privacy of the event which saved many lives.

He used to appoint his deputy whenever leaving for any campaign. At the occasion of Uhad, he was not extremely far from the city, but he kept vulnerable people like women and children intact and appointed his deputy. So, delegated his authority. He appointed Abu Bakker (RA) the leader of the hajji and nominated him his successor. Abu Bakker (RA) lead slat and the prophet (ﷺ) prayed behind him.

He did not try to confront the opponents directly in most of his life. At the time of his Hijrah, he had avoided the enemy which proved useful because he reached Madinah safely which was his objective. Prior to Hodabia treaty, the enemy purpose was to stop Muslims forcefully, but the prophet (ﷺ) did not offer them the opportunity. He changed the famous way of caravans and used side path to avoid Quraysh. The Hodabia truce was itself an example of it despite his colleagues were ready to do anything he would ask them. He tried to convince Jews/Banu Nazir to honour treaty to avoid any armed encounter. Even at the time of conquering of Makkah, the first condition he put to Quraysh was to pay a ransom of the Khazai's killed people.

The prophet (ﷺ) managed through clearly defined objectives. He said to the nearest effect that he had been sent to convey the message of Allah, the exalted. His objective also included the welfare of human being. He said to the nearest effect that he was a plain warner to everyone. He wanted to save people from the Fire of Hell. He said to proclaim the oneness of Allah (SWT) you will be successful. Thus, the prophet (ﷺ) had shown the way of success in the world and in the Hereafter.

The prophet's (ﷺ)plans were *flexible* which means they could accommodate changes as and when required. When we look at the Hodabia treaty, there were no intentions of war but as soon as the situation changed preparation was made to get ready for it. All the companions were ready to fight despite they were not equipped with the necessary hardware required for a battle.

An analogous situation happened at the occasion of Badr; the prophet (ﷺ) was following a trade caravan which ran away out of their reach. The prophet (ﷺ) and companions prepared themselves for a small encounter with the security personnel of the caravan but plan were changed to fight a full-fledged war. The war was the first of its nature and the troops were not fully ready for it. But the plan was adjusted according to the situation of the time.

The prophet (ﷺ)was always *determined* to achieve his goals. For example, on Uhad, the young people suggested to go out of the city but most of the mature were in favour of staying in the city. The prophet (ﷺ) armed himself and came out of his residence meanwhile the young companions knew that the prophet (ﷺ) wanted to stay in Madinah. They changed their minds and wanted to stay in Madinah, but the prophet (ﷺ) replied, it was not appropriate for a prophet (ﷺ) to unarmed himself. But the decision was a success.

Finance

The prophet (ﷺ) had financed all the major projects through self-financed or volunteer sources because the department of finance did not exist by that time. Later, the development came into being and zakat and Usher were introduced.

His Hijrah was the first occasion when material resources were required. He bought a she-camel for his transport. One purpose of integration (creation of brotherhood between Helpers and Migrants) was to arrange financial resources for the migrants because they did not bring their belongings to Madinah.

All the wars were financed through the general contribution from the public. However, he borrowed supplies and weapons from eminent people before the battle of Honain. The development of finance was established later for which the collector of Zakat was appointed. While spoils of wars were distributed for needy people. One of the uses of taxes (Zakat, spoils of war etc) was winning the hearts. The prophet (ﷺ) had bestowed upon the eminent people of Quraysh out of the spoils of war of Honain after conquered of Makkah.

As a manager of finance, one must create sources of finance, apply, and distribute them prudently. He also keeps them in a safe place so that they may be available when required. The prophet (ﷺ) had defined the sources of funding i.e. volunteer sources, taxes etc. He had distributed justly. Once his dearest daughter, Fatimah (RA) visited him to ask for a slave or maid because she used to do all her household jobs herself which made her tied. The prophet (ﷺ) bestows her famous *Tasbeehaat Fatimah* but said there were more deserved people waiting for the slaves.

Human resources

For him, people were the most valuable resource. Allah (SWT) ordained him when your colleagues make a mistake, you forgive them, repent to Allah (SWT) for them and consult them.[12] He had implemented these principles at all occasions, performed HR (Human Resource) functions as an expert, made appointments on the basis of merit. He appointed Abu Bakker (RA) as his successor because he sacrificed the most, he was knowledgeable and calm in temperament. He trained his colleagues on daily basis. The beauty of his management style was that whoever entered his religion he seldom left it, his "organisation".

The prophet (ﷺ) was a patience administrator. He has never shown impatience or panic. Always remain calm and cool in extreme circumstances

---

[12] Al-e-Imran: 159.

either in distress or happiness. He was extremely under pressure in the journey of Taif but remained calm and did not take any emotional decision. Similarly, during Hijrah, in Badr, Uhad, and Honain his temperament was exemplary. He was a man of patience when dealing with his colleagues. At the occasion of Hodabia, the companions were upset because he accepted all the unfavourable conditions of infidels. But he managed the crisis successfully. Again, at the conquered of Makkah, the Helpers were not comfortable about the distribution of spoils of war, but he managed the situation.

The prophet (ﷺ) did not argue with his opponents or his companions. Whenever someone tried to argue with him, he simply read the Quran or invited to him to Islam. It suggests that he used to apply the positive approach to address various issues. Similarly, he never criticises his companions; when a companion sent a letter to his family about the intentions of Muslims before taking over Makkah, he did not reprimand him. According to Molana Saad (Damat berkato hu) when a colleague makes a mistake, the leader or other involved in the situation should remember his previous work and sacrifice for Islam. The prophet (ﷺ) said about him that Allah, the exalted, has forgiven prior or forthcoming mistakes of all those who participated in Badr.

The prophet (ﷺ) also encouraged mediations to resolve various problems because it is a peaceful way to address human issues. He sent Usman bin Affan (RA) as a mediator to Makkah to talk to Quraysh about the matter now of Hodabia. He also appointed a mediator to decide the fate of a Jewish tribe; the Jews suggested the mediator and he accepted it.

His entire management strategy was based on the application of peaceful means. The enemy had initiated the three major armed encounters and accumulated a bundle of crimes so that the root of the campaign must be eliminated. The Makkah initiative was the answer to their consecutive attempts to eliminate the Islamic state. But the history is witnessed that it prevailed peace in the entire Araba world because most of the Arabs remained indifferent in the struggle and principally, they were peaceful. As a planner, the prophet (ﷺ) was a reactive manager in terms of war, but he was the proactive planner for spreading peace. Islam is a message of peace. At one time, the peace was the rule of the game, a woman travelled alone while she was wearing silver and gold from Yemen to Makkah, but no one hurt her. He planned the journey of Taif, Hijrah, and truce with Quraysh, Jews and other Arabs for the cause of peace and to integrate scattered tribes.

He planned and managed business intelligence systematically. At Hijrah, he had appointed Abdullah bin Abu Bakker (RA) to visit the city daily and gather information. He was delivering it to the noble team in the evening. The truce of Mina was signed in tight security; the Quraysh could not smell it and even the infidels of Madinah could not know what had happened. Had it not signed the treaty the Hijrah was not possible which became the beginning of Islamic revolution. The security was also kept at "red alert" level at the occasion of conquered of Makkah. It not only made the opponents unaware of what was happening in Madinah but also saved bloodshed during the combat.

The basis of the above-mentioned security/business intelligence was the communication system. The prophet (ﷺ) had developed the communication system very strongly right from the beginning of his revolution. He always kept an eye on the political or other movements of his opponents. Quraysh held a meeting of their so-called parliament about his martyr before Hijrah. He responded immediately and decided to leave Makkah. Consequently, Quraysh could not implement their vicious plan. He remained aware of the activities of Jews, Quraysh, and other Arabs while in Madinah. He had defined a system for it. He sent an informer to know what was happening in the battle of Trench. The informer told him that they were bored and unhappy about the developments. And they wanted to leave. At the occasion of Honain, the prophet (ﷺ) sent an informer who stayed many days among the opponents and explained the situation to him.

Bibliography

Adair, John (2010) The Leadership of Muhammad (pbuh), New Delhi: Kogan Page India Private Limited.

Al-Bahaqi, Abi Bakker Ahmad Al-Hussain (2009) Dhalail Al-Nabuwwa, Karachi: Dharul Ishaat.

DeCenzo, David A. and Stephen P. Robbins (2010) Human Resource Management, New York: John Wiley & Sons.

Iqbal, Javed, and Muhammad Mushtaq Ahmad (2009) Planning in the Islamic Tradition: The Case of Hijrah Expedition, INSIGHTS 01(3), 37-68.

Kaandhlawi, Muhammad Zakarya (1997), Fazail-e-Amaal, Lahore: Kutibkhana Faizi.

Koontz, Harold, and Heinz Weihrich (2006) Essentials of Management, New Delhi: Tata McGraw-Hill Education, pp. 81-84.

Lings, M M (1994) Muhammad, his life based on the earliest sources, Lahore: Suhail Academy.

Mubarakpuri, Safiur Rahman (1995) "The Sealed Nectar" (Ar-Raheeq Al-Makhtum), Lahore: Al-Maktba Alsalfia.

Nadvi, Sulaiman Hussaini (2205) Khutbat-e-Seerat, Karachi: Zam-Zam Publishers.

Noamani, Shibli and Syed Solaiman Nadhvi (2004) Seeratun-Nabi, Karachi: Dharul-Ishaat.

Phalwari, Muhammad Jaafer (1995) Peghambr-e-Insaniat, Lahore: Idara Sakafat-e-Islamia.

Robbins, Stephen and Mary Coulter (2011) Management, New Delhi: Pearson Education.

Siddiqi, Naeem (1997) The Benefactor of Humanity (Mohsin-e-Insaniyat), Dehli: Markazi Matabah Islami Publishers.

Index

Abdurehman bin Aof (RA), *80*
Abu Bakker, *9, 14, 15, 21, 67, 82, 93, 108, 115*
Abu Sufyan, *33, 72, 120*
Abuzer (RA), *42*
Abyssinia, *14, 25, 26, 27, 30, 45, 59, 62, 79, 80, 92, 93, 106*
Adham (AS), *95*
Ali (RA), *103, 121*
Allah, xv
Allah (SWT), *3, 14, 16, 19, 35, 36, 41, 42, 43, 44, 45, 47, 51, 81, 106*
Aows, *29, 60, 69, 98*
Arqum (RA), *18, 19*
Badr, *10, 21, 22, 26, 33, 40, 50, 73, 75, 83, 110, 111, 117*
bait-e-uqba Saniya, *28*
Banu Nazeer, *86*
Bilal (RA), *13*
book, *152*
books, *155*
case study, *154*
change, *154*
Comparing alternatives courses, *89*
Decenzo, *11, 40*
Hamzah (RA), *61, 62*
Helpers, *26, 28, 31, 48, 49, 68, 71, 73, 74, 96, 97*
hijrah, *14, 25, 65, 89, 90, 91, 97, 108, 115, 129, 137, 138*
Hijrah, *6, 30, 47, 65, 106*
Hodabia, *xviii, 26, 35, 36, 51, 55, 71, 72, 75, 83, 93, 102, 103, 111, 112, 117, 120, 126, 127, 129, 130, 135, 136*
Honain, *117, 118, 133, 135, 139*
Human Resource, *134*
Integration, *26, 31, 48, 67, 95, 97*
Iqbal, **i, ii, xx**
Iqbal and Ahmad (2009), *6, 25, 65, 90, 105, 108*

Islamic, *2, 3, 22, 48, 72, 110*
Khalid bin Waleed, *94*
khams, *119*
Khizraj, *29, 69*
king of Persia, *47*
Knootz and Weihrich, 2006, *109*
Madinah, *xviii, 6, 8, 10, 12, 13, 25, 26, 27, 28, 29, 30, 33, 46, 47, 48, 49, 50, 51, 53, 65, 67, 68, 69, 70, 72, 73, 74, 85, 86, 90, 91, 98, 101, 102, 103, 110, 111, 128, 129, 132, 137, 138*
Makkah, *xviii, 4, 6, 8, 9, 13, 20, 26, 27, 28, 30, 31, 35, 36, 39, 51, 52, 55, 57, 60, 67, 72, 74, 75, 79, 81, 82, 89, 90, 92, 93, 94, 99, 103, 107, 111, 117, 118, 128, 130, 133, 135, 136, 138*
Makken, *12, 13*
management, *6, 7, 11, 12, 20, 30, 40, 53, 118*
Management, *154*
Managers, *154*
Masjid, *18*

Molana Mubarikpuri (1995), *67*
Molana Saad, *135*
Molana Shibli, *109, 118*
Muhammad, *153, 154*
Muslims, *4, 9, 14, 22, 27, 29, 34, 35, 36, 39, 46, 47, 51, 52, 53, 55, 59, 64, 67, 68, 70, 72, 73, 74, 76, 77, 79, 80, 93, 94, 100, 101, 102, 106, 107, 110, 111*
Nomani and Nadvi, *119, 120*
objectives, *12, 13, 39, 40, 42, 45, 51, 52, 53, 81, 91, 92, 93*
planning, *1, 2, 5, 6, 8, 11, 12, 22, 25, 30, 36, 37, 40, 57, 58, 89, 105, 153*
Planning, *152*
Planning characteristics, *125*
Plans, *5, 105, 115*
Prophet, *153*
prophet (ﷺ), *2, 3, 4, 6, 12, 13, 14, 15, 18, 20, 27, 29, 39, 40, 41, 42, 45, 59, 60, 65, 71, 77, 79, 80, 81, 89, 92, 97,*

100, 106, 107, 108, 109, 110, 111, 115, 117, 118
Prophet (ﷺ), *151, 152, 153*
Quantification, *117*
Quran, *98*
Quraysh, *15, 21, 22, 27, 29, 33, 34, 35, 36, 45, 47, 49, 50, 51, 53, 55, 59, 60, 61, 71, 73, 74, 75, 76, 81, 82, 83, 85, 93, 94, 98, 101, 102, 108, 110, 111, 128, 129, 133, 136, 137, 138*
Risk, *154*
Robins and Coulter, *11*
Robins and Coutler, *11*
Saad bin Maaz (RA), *74, 98*

Sallaabee (2006), *51*
supporting plans, *106, 108, 111, 115*
Tabuk, *10, 22, 101, 116*
Taif, *27, 30, 37, 38, 54, 55, 81, 99*
Taif, treaty, *126*
Treaty of Mina, *46, 62*
Truce with Jews, *26, 32, 49, 111*
Uhad, *22, 85, 92, 101, 112, 117, 129, 131, 135*
Umer (RA), *19, 21, 62, 67*
Usman bin Affan (RA), *79, 110, 112*
vision, *3*
war of Trench, *39, 100*
Yasrib, *28, 60*

About the author

Dr. Javed Iqbal belongs to Rawalakot district Poonch Azad Kashmir. He received his early education from Pilot High School Rawalakot and received his matriculation in 1975 and intermediate from Hussain Shaheed Degree College of the same town. He earned BBA with a gold medal and an MBA with a gold medal from Azad Jammu and Kashmir University in 1986. He was appointed as a lecturer in Business Administration in the same university. Later, he was selected by the government of Pakistan for higher studies and deputed to the United Kingdom. He received MBA from the University of Hull and Ph.D. from the University of Salford. Dr. Iqbal has been working in England in various capacities: professor, director of studies, marketing advisor and academic advisor. Dr. Iqbal returned to Home in 2006 and joined Iqra University Islamabad campus as an associate professor. He became the head of the department of technology Management in International Islamic University Islamabad (IIUI). He went back to England for some time and re-joined IIUI in 2012. He joined AKU (AJ&K) as professor and Dean Faculty of Management Sciences in March 2015.

He is a distinguished teacher and world known scholar. His article title "Learning from a Doctoral Research Project: Structure and Content of a Research Proposal" has been classed by one of the professors as the best piece of knowledge for doctoral students at Deakin University in Australia. This paper is widely used and referred all over the world. Dr. Javed Iqbal has been nominated by an international organization for the Award of Distinguished Scientist for his research contribution this year. His books on various subjects are available on amazon. His poetry is to be published soon as well.

Other books by the author (s)

1. Prof Dr. Javed Iqbal Saani (2018) Managerial Implications of Hijrah Expedition, Intellectual Capital Enterprise Limited, London, available on Amazon (Paperback edition)
2. Prof Dr. Javed Iqbal Saani (2018) Managerial Implications of Battle of BADR, Intellectual Capital Enterprise Limited, London, available on Amazon (Paperback edition)
3. Prof Dr. Javed Iqbal Saani (2018) Managerial Thoughts of the Prophet (ﷺ), Intellectual Capital Enterprise Limited, London, available on Amazon (Paperback edition)
4. Prof Dr. Javed Iqbal Saani (2018) Controlling Strategy of the Prophet (ﷺ), Intellectual Capital Enterprise Limited, London, available on Amazon (Paperback edition)
5. Prof Dr. Javed Iqbal Saani (2018) Leading Strategy of the Prophet (ﷺ), Intellectual Capital

Enterprise Limited, London, available on Amazon (Paperback edition)

6. Prof Dr. Javed Iqbal Saani (2018) Organising Strategy of the Prophet (ﷺ), Intellectual Capital Enterprise Limited, London, available on Amazon (Paperback edition)

7. Prof Dr. Javed Iqbal Saani (2018) Planning Strategy of the Prophet (ﷺ), Intellectual Capital Enterprise Limited, London, available on Amazon (Paperback edition)

8. Prof Dr. Javed Iqbal Saani (2018) Qualities of Momins: The Quranic Perspective, Intellectual Capital Enterprise Limited, London, available on Amazon (Paperback edition)

9. Prof Dr. Javed Iqbal Saani (2018) Hajj Experience: Combining Dawah and Manasiks, Intellectual Capital Enterprise Limited, London, available on Amazon (Paperback edition)

10. Prof Dr. Javed Iqbal Saani (2018) Sukhn-e-Saani (The book of poetry), Intellectual Capital Enterprise Limited, London, available on Amazon (Paperback edition)

11. Prof Dr. Javed Iqbal Saani (2018) Managing Your Projects, Intellectual Capital Enterprise Limited, London, available on amazon.co.uk. (Paperback edition)

12. Prof Dr. Javed Iqbal Saani (2017) Business Case Studies, Intellectual Capital Enterprise Limited, London, available on Amazon (Paperback edition)

13. Prof Dr. Javed Iqbal Saani (2017) Virtues of Sickness: Selected Ahadith, available on Amazon (Paperback edition)

14. Prof Dr. Javed Iqbal Saani (2017) Prophet (ﷺ) Muhammad (ﷺ) as a planning expert, available on Amazon (Paperback edition)

15. Prof Dr. Javed Iqbal Saani (2017) Muhammad (ﷺ): His Trials & Tribulations, available on Amazon (Paperback edition)

16. Prof Dr. Javed Iqbal Saani (2017) Sales and Marketing: Selected Ahadith, available on amazon.co.uk. (Paperback edition)

17. Prof Dr. Prof Dr. Javed Iqbal Saani (2016) Research Proposals: Contents & Exemplars, available on amazon.co.uk. (Paperback edition)

18. Prof Dr. Javed Iqbal Saani (2016) Responsibilities of Managers: Selected Ahadith, available on amazon.co.uk. (Paperback edition)

19. Prof Dr. Javed Iqbal Saani (2016) Experience: The Journey of My Life, available on amazon.co.uk. (Paperback edition)

20. Prof Dr. Javed Iqbal Saani (2012) Understanding Information Systems, Manchester: GRaASS.

21. Prof Dr Javed Iqbal Saani (2011) Digital Divide in South Asia ISBN: 9789699578120.

22. Prof Dr. Javed Iqbal Saani and Muhammad Rafi Khattak (2011) Managing Risk in Projects, ISBN: 9789699578090.

23. Prof Dr. Javed Iqbal Saani and Muhammad Nadeem Khan (2011, 2018) Understanding Project Management, ISBN: 978969957845, available on Amazon (Paperback edition)

24. Prof Dr. Javed Iqbal Saani (2011) Information Systems for Managers, Grass Books, Manchester.

25. Prof Dr. Javed Iqbal Saani (2010) Managing strategic change: a real-world case study, ISBN:

978-3838330952, available on amazon.co.uk. (Paperback edition)

Notes

www.ingramcontent.com/pod-product-compliance
Lightning Source LLC
Chambersburg PA
CBHW020656220526
45464CB00001B/456